Also by Sanae Ishida

Sewing Books

----

*Animal Friends to Sew: Simple Handmade
Decor, Toys, and Gifts for Kids*

*Sewing Happiness: A Year of Simple
Projects for Living Well*

Little Kunoichi the Ninja Girl
Picture Book Series

Ba-Chan the Ninja Grandma
Chibi Samurai Wants a Pet
Little Kunoichi the Ninja Girl

Little Sumo Board Book Series

Sumo Colors
Sumo Counting
Sumo Opposites
Sumo Shapes

sewing love

HANDMADE CLOTHES FOR ANY BODY

SANAE ISHIDA

Photography by Manuela Insixiengmay and Amy Johnson
Styling by Rachel Grunig

SASQUATCH BOOKS
SEATTLE

Printed in China

SASQUATCH BOOKS with colophon is a registered trademark of Penguin Random House LLC

26 25 24 23 22   9 8 7 6 5 4 3 2 1

Editor: Hannah Elnan / Production editor: Bridget Sweet
Designer: Anna Goldstein / Production designer: Alison Keefe
Illustrations: Sanae Ishida / Photography: Manuela Insixiengmay (pages viii, x, 14–35, 52, 64, 76, 96, 105, 126, 148, 168, 173–174, 180, 199, 202, 207, 212, 229–230, 248, 260, and 270), Amy Johnson (pages ii, 38, 43–44, 125, 131, 138, 140, 146, 149, 155, 157, 163, 165, 171, 175, 181–182, 190, 193, 200, 203, 210, 213, 220, 223, 231, 233, 239–240, 247, 249, 257, and 272) and Lauren Segal (pages vi, xv, and 260) / Styling: Rachel Grunig
Hair and makeup styling: Kaija Towner / Models: M (pages 14, 23, 126, and 230), Amy Johnson (pages 15, 32–33, and 168), K (pages 16–17, 21, 27, 173, 180, 199, and 270), Sanae (pages xv, 17, 24–25, 28, 52, and 270), Melizza Rosich (pages viii, 18, 22, and 148), Wendee Wieking (pages 19, 31, 212, 229, and 248), Rachel Grunig (pages 20, 29, and 202), Mimi Santos (pages 26, 35, and 174), and Natasha Alphonse (pages 30 and 34).

Library of Congress Cataloging-in-Publication Data
Names: Ishida, Sanae, author.
Title: Sewing love : handmade clothes for any body / Sanae Ishida.
Description: Seattle : Sasquatch Books, [2022] | Includes index.
Identifiers: LCCN 2021024200 | ISBN 9781632172815 (paperback) | ISBN 9781632172822 (ebook)
Subjects: LCSH: Sewing.
Classification: LCC TT705 .I76 2022 | DDC 646/.1--dc23
LC record available at https://lccn.loc.gov/2021024200

ISBN: 978-1-63217-281-5

Sasquatch Books / 1325 Fourth Avenue, Suite 1025 / Seattle, WA 98101

SasquatchBooks.com

For Annelieke

5½ x 2 = 11"
REDUCED BY ANOTHER 3/8" ON EACH SIDE
modified Armscye
UNDERARM BRING IN AND UP FOR FRONT + BACK
TANK #2 PROTOTYPE
WAISTLINE

Contents

Project List

Where It All Started

A LITTLE OVER TEN YEARS AGO, I was hunched over my desk at work with my nose practically pressed against a gigantic computer monitor, my pregnant bod squeezed into what felt like a very small cubicle, as I scrolled through garment-sewing blogs. (I was taking a very long "lunch break" from my mind-numbing corporate job.) After what might have been hours of diving down that particular online rabbit hole, my brain combusted with the thought: *Sewing completely changes your relationship with your body.* I saw women from all over the world, confidently and generously sharing photos of beautiful clothes they'd made with their own hands to fit their one-of-a-kind bodies. I read how they felt liberated from fashion trends, how sewing connected them to their bodies in a whole new way, and how empowering the act of making clothes can be. The message was clear: sewing is life-changing. At the time, I didn't even own a sewing machine. Yet I knew in the core of my soul that this correlation between sewing and clothes and body image was significant, and I wanted to be a part of it.

At that point, I was nearly nine months into pregnancy and had been feeling especially delicate about my morphing physique—which was saying something for someone who had struggled mightily with weight for decades. And was it my imagination, or was that alarm in my husband's eyes as my body grew and grew and grew? Baby-making amped up my appetite, and I had gained sixty pounds. People constantly asked, "Are you expecting twins?" When the time finally came to pop out the bebé, my daughter would turn out to be a wisp of a thing, weighing in at six pounds, eight ounces. I had apparently consumed fifty-three and a half pounds worth of croissants and ice cream throughout the gestation period.

Back in my cube, I shifted uncomfortably and adjusted my belly as I continued to read the blog posts about this radical connection between sewing and body acceptance. It wasn't that garment sewing transforms the body to appear gorgeous, but I was getting the feeling that the secret sauce was in learning how to appreciate the body as is, deeply and unequivocally. What I felt for my own body at that moment was the very opposite of appreciation: disappointment, shame, hostility.

Sewing could change that? I was in!

However, it took many years and many excuses before I actually began sewing clothes for myself. Sewing seemed hard. I felt lazy. I didn't know where to start exactly, and that uncertainty kept me stuck. But when I finally revved up the sewing machine and started to practice making tops and dresses and pants and so much more for my unique body, I got it. I *really* got it. Learning how to make clothes that truly fit *me*—in every sense—was nothing short of revolutionary. I was in my late thirties when I started this adventure, and up to that point, I'd spent the better part of my life loathing my body, trying to sculpt it into a shape that I thought would make me acceptable to myself and others. Sewing fundamentally shifted my attitude toward myself, and I stopped trying to change my appearance to fit into some unattainable ideal mold. I created clothes that felt good to wear *and* made me feel beautiful—and sewing became an act of kindness and nurturing for myself.

I created this book with my former self in mind: a procrastinator, full of excuses, excited by the prospect of sewing up some love for myself, but unsure of how to begin. I don't regret the path I took to get here, since I learned a lot along the way, but it would have been really nice to have had a simple, encouraging book to start with. So many of the sewing books I read provided technical skills and techniques (in perhaps too much detail) but rarely addressed the psychological discomforts of sewing clothes for ourselves, or the overwhelm of navigating the many pattern and fabric options. They seemed to brush over the angst I felt about my body when they'd casually recommend that I "find a friend to measure all the body parts." *What?! I could never do that! I don't even want to measure myself!* My resistance was immense. And so I kept putting off sewing clothes for myself.

Many of the books also made pattern-drafting sound intimidating and exacting, using words like "difficult" and "complicated," citing discouraging examples of people trying to draft the perfect pants pattern for thirty years and still failing. Drafting and fitting don't need to be so complex. A few years ago, my mom (an artist and veteran sewer) watched me carefully trace a pattern from a Japanese craft book, add the seam allowances, and assemble the pieces. She was impressed, but also puzzled. "I've never used a commercial pattern," she informed me. "You just need a few measurements, some paper to sketch out the necessary pieces, adjust a bit as you go, and it ends up fitting just fine, you know?" I wasn't confident enough to try it at the time, but as always, Mama was right.

I want to share all that I've learned and save you some time with this book. With that in mind, I did my best to simplify every project. Whether you've never even looked at a sewing machine or you've been sewing for decades, my aim is to include helpful advice and (I hope) inspiring projects for truly customizable wardrobe basics within these pages. You'll find:

- the story of my evolution from the self-conscious queen of procrastination to someone who can whip up a custom-tailored top in an afternoon, and the lessons I learned along the way.
- a "lookbook" showcasing all of the projects in the book, worn by people with a variety of body types.
- a section that covers the foundational knowledge you need to get started, from sewing basics and tools to a step-by-step guide to creating your own slopers, which will be the building blocks for drafting your own patterns to fit your unique shape. Think of the sloper as a 2-D version of a dress form. It's essentially your singular body shape translated onto a flat piece of paper, and you can use it to create any pattern you like. Common fit issues will also be addressed in this section.

- project instructions for fifteen versatile garments with detailed illustrations along with options for variations and quick overviews of useful techniques. The slopers you create will enable you to draft any project in this book—and beyond. Your body and your preferences for style and fit may change over time, but once you have the sloper know-how, you'll be able to create the wardrobe of your dreams at any stage in your life.

This book, at heart, is about starting exactly where we are. Starting is always the hardest part (followed by the close second and third of continuing and finishing). My call to action is always, "If I can do it, anyone can!" I'm still not an expert at sewing or fitting. I am, however, becoming an expert at understanding myself, at paying attention to what feels right for me, inside and out. For me, sewing has been a creative expedition of discovery that continues to uplift me, but more than anything else, it has been a way to learn how to become friendly with my body. My body had felt like a punishment for so long, and I was bone-tired of it all. Those sewing bloggers that I discovered a decade ago knew what they were talking about. Sewing has *completely* changed the way I view my body. Not only that, it's changed the way I treat my body for the better. There were a few big hurdles to leap over, for sure, but I worked steadily to accept this human mass of neurons and tissues and muscles and pumping, thriving blood. And then—I started to *like* it. These days, I unapologetically love my body and revel in the life-giving miracle that it is. My body is beautiful, and so is yours. Truly. My deepest hope is that this book will be the gentle, loving booster that propels you to create clothing that embodies and expresses *you*. I've endeavored to make the process as simple as possible. So let's do this.

the love story

(clockwise from left) My mom's first art show in America. She made almost everything in the photo, including the floral hat that my dad is wearing, which is my favorite.

The pièce de résistance of the overalls that my mom sewed is clearly the bunny appliqué.

Me circa 1975, sporting a handmade bikini. My mom was not one for following conventions.

A Life in Clothes

I'VE ALWAYS ADORED CLOTHES. Obsessed over them, really. At the tender age of twelve, I started going to the local library every chance I could find to pore over issues of *Vogue* and *Seventeen*. I frequently checked out the back issues to take home with me and scrutinized all the Dos and Don'ts, mentally stockpiling the information for the day when I could actually choose and buy my own clothing. My mom had been sewing my clothes since I was an infant; she was partial to brightly colored, outrageously patterned outfits, and by middle school, I was having none of that. Because family funds were tight, I was then stuck with Goodwill finds and hand-me-downs from my mom's petite friend. This friend was a professional violinist for the local orchestra whose tastes vacillated between "Bohemian" and "insurance agency receptionist"—think flowy fabrics and frills, blazers and pencil skirts. And back when I was a kid, thrift stores left a lot to be desired in the youth fashion department. Despite my best efforts, I wasn't able to pull off any of the looks offered up to me. I still vividly remember the humiliation of wearing an ill-fitting white silk blouse and black skirt in the eighth grade. The high-necked frilly white blouse gave me the air of a tragic Victorian character, and the skirt was a little too big for me. It kept sliding down, and I was terrified that I would flash my underwear in the middle school cafeteria. I simply looked out of place. The clothes felt *wrong*. All I wanted was to look like everyone else, like I belonged. I stared longingly at the other girls' Guess jeans with the tiny zippers at the ankles. I wondered how much those unisex ID# shirts cost, the ones with a boxy fit and funky designs and a chest pocket with the little "ID#" label. And don't get me started on the Michael Jackson phase that my mom went through, when she forced my brothers and me to wear matching T-shirts from which MJ's sparkly smile radiated from our chests. The early '80s were rough for me.

I couldn't wait for high school, and I counted down the days till I could sign up for a work permit and finally make all of my fashion dreams come true. I turned fifteen. Got the permit. Found a job (I sold shoes at a small tennis shop). Bought the clothes. There was only one problem.

I hated my body.

All this time, I'd thought it was the secondhand clothes that were the issue. I had assumed that once I acquired the clothes I liked, I would start looking like the models in all the magazines I studied obsessively. Never mind that most of the models were six feet tall and one hundred pounds and white. In the glaring lights of fitting rooms, my Asian facial features crumpled in disappointment as I gazed at my reflection. The Guess jeans got stuck at my voluptuous calves, and when I found a size that could handle my lower legs, the waist gaped, and I could have easily popped in a couple of cantaloupes in the space allotted for the booty. The supposedly ankle-length hem dragged on the floor—I cursed my genetics that generated such short legs. I'd also developed into quite a buxom lass for my frame, and I couldn't find tops that didn't transform me into a cleavage-parading seductress. When I tried to hide my bosom in loose-fitting garments, I looked like an aspiring body builder. And if the fitting room mirrors were anything to go by, I was obviously chubby and out of shape. I felt ugly.

So, naturally, I became a shopaholic. For much of my life, my hero's journey centered around finding a pair of jeans that fit like a glove and tops that would accentuate my figure, but somehow deter sleazy men. I worried that this was a vain and shallow pursuit, but I was addicted and I blazed on, credit card at the ready. My quest took me into every apparel store in the Los Angeles metro area and beyond, and my closet was bursting with the ill-fitting clothes I left in my wake. In a vague sort of way, it occurred to me that there was something wrong in assuming that I would feel better when I finally had the right jeans, but I wasn't about to give up.

The Holy Grail was out there; it had to be. My overstuffed closet indicated otherwise.

As my dream wardrobe remained elusive, my attention gradually shifted to trying to change my body instead. I starved it, forced down unappealing food combinations at specific times with militaristic precision, pumped it full of diet pills. I was both the torturer and the tortured as I pummeled my body with criticism and then begged it to please, please stop expanding.

My food intake and fitness regimen were particularly amplified during my college years. Ironically, I was fitting in for the first time, since I was surrounded by other girls just like me, trying to live up to the prescribed societal ideal of beauty.

I remember, in particular, a girl who lived on my dorm floor. She was such an extreme example of the pervasive preoccupation with the body, it was hard not to pay attention to her. She was thin, painfully so. Her clavicles were razor sharp, and her knees seemed disproportionately large on her legs. She maintained her low body weight by attending aerobics classes twice a day and subsisting on lettuce. Her face was mottled with cystic acne that she covered with thick layers of foundation, and she endlessly talked about how fat she was. I was becoming familiar with this sort of behavior because it was so prevalent on campus. Everywhere I turned, I saw my fellow collegiate gals forsaking food, or binging and purging, or working out nonstop, or some combination thereof. Eating disorders seemed utterly normal, and I participated in my own way with intense diets.

Amid the throngs of the body and food obsessed, I had a lovely friend who stood out in a different way. I'll call her Shelly. We met in the beginning of the school year when we were both sophomores. She was a plump, adorable young woman from Hawaii with a lilting, melodic way of speaking. Always ready with a bright smile, she had a laidback openness about her, like a surfer yogi. I immediately felt comfortable around her; she radiated a sense of peace. As I got to know her, I noticed that she started showing up with a large water bottle from which she sipped frequently. She would order healthy salads and lean meats whenever we had lunch at one of the campus eateries, and she would enjoy a little dessert afterward. Then she began sporting running shorts, and by the time spring quarter rolled around, she was slim, trim, and *totally* hot. All the while, she remained jovial and darling as ever, and I don't recall a single time she complained about . . . anything, really. I was powerfully curious to know what her weight loss secret was. More than that, I wanted to know how she was so ridiculously happy all the time. She hadn't seemed all that bothered when she had some extra weight on her body, and she seemed equally delighted when she became a doppelganger for Cindy Crawford (remember, it was the '90s).

I never asked her how she did it, because I was too afraid that I would sound as desperate as I felt. I didn't want anyone to know how much I wanted to lose weight, how much I abhorred my body. It wasn't really the weight loss or health secrets that I craved, however. Ultimately, I yearned to find out how she seemed to genuinely like herself, no matter what. *That's* what I wanted.

\ı\ı\ıı\ııı\ııı\ıııı\ıııı\ıııı\ııı\ıı\ı\ı

"Have you gained weight? You look heavier. How much do you weigh, anyway?"

The utterer of these skewering words peered up at me with kindly eyes full of curiosity. I was in my mid-twenties, living and teaching English in Japan, and the locals peppered me with these types of inquiries *all the time*. Another incident involved a luncheon with my Japanese colleagues at a nearby restaurant. When the hostess led us to our table, my colleagues immediately scurried about, moving one of the tables farther away from the wall. "What are you doing?" I asked, confused. "We're making more room for you," one of the teachers replied, patting me gently on the shoulder. The implication was evident: I was too big to fit in the space for "normal" people. My face turned the color of the outfit I was wearing, a loose, dark pink romper-type thing with culottes that looked like a dress. I reluctantly plunked myself down in the designated chair. It was undeniable that I was larger than the average Japanese woman (even though I am Japanese American). I was accustomed to purchasing a medium size in the US, but in Japan I was mortified to find myself digging through the extra-large bins and still coming up empty.

I've thought a lot about those moments in Japan in the last decades. For my Japanese friends, there was no reason to hide how much they weighed. It was just a number, after all. And it was out of consideration and a sincere desire for me to be comfortable that they moved the table. Again and again though, I replayed memories like these and sunk deeper into a sense of not-enough-ness that warped my view of my body.

I also reinforced my body dysmorphia with an intense focus on clothing sizes. There was this one time when I needed a new pair of pants in my pre-sewing days. I was back in the US, and it was such a relief to find more clothing options. I went into a store and grabbed a few pairs in my regular size. Just for giggles, I also plucked a pair that was two sizes smaller. I tried on the smaller size first and I barely squeezed in. *Barely*. And you know what? I bought those pants. I managed to sort of waddle in them, and sitting was absolutely out of the question, but I was so elated that they zipped up all the way that I convinced myself that at some point, I would be thin enough to exhale while wearing them. The pants never saw the light of day, and eventually I donated them. A tiny little number on a tiny little tag held the power to simultaneously elevate and destroy my sense of self-worth.

Fast forward many years to when I sat in my claustrophobic cubicle at work, gobbling up blog posts about sewing and body positivity. A few weeks later, I would find myself writhing and gripping the back of a booth in a pancake house across the street from the hospital, waiting for my cervix to dilate. At 6:21 p.m. that evening, my child emerged. I remember gazing down at my newborn daughter and wanting so very much to create beautiful tiny things for her. As I navigated new motherhood, sewing became a sanity-preserving outlet, and I stitched up an outfit or a toy here and there, sewing into the mysterious hours of the night when time loses all meaning. As I pumped out itty-bitty dresses, sometimes I fantasized about sewing for myself as well, but I always put it off. My body just wasn't thin enough yet.

Then, in 2011, I was diagnosed with a chronic autoimmune condition called Graves' disease. At my worst, I was bedridden, had gained over twenty pounds in rapid succession, and for a long time I sported one odd black eye and a pallor that my mom dubbed "Phantom of the Opera." I also felt terribly, terribly sorry for myself. Graves' is marked by hyperthyroidism, which means that my thyroid gets out of whack and overproduces hormones. This often results in symptoms like goiters, bugged-out eyes, and massive anxiety. Luckily, I didn't develop a lumpy throat or buggy eyes, but I did experience off-the-charts anxiety and had the tendency to catch every virus in the air.

But one of the major benefits of getting diagnosed with a potentially fatal disease is the direct confrontation with mortality. Suddenly, all the small fears are laughable. Life is suddenly precious, and you don't have time to be messing around with whether your calves are too big or what other people think of you. When I was in the throes of my illness and hyperfocused on getting better, I noticed that I hardly procrastinated, which was very out of character for me. And because my energy reserves were severely limited, I was very conscientious about spending my time on things that actually mattered. I stopped putting off enjoying my family and reading good books and taking care of my body. And I dove into sewing, for the pure joy of it.

I promised myself I'd sew something for my daughter from my numerous Japanese craft books every week for a full year because I wanted to master sewing, to be able to say, "I can make anything." Week after week, I created little outfits, and I noticed that all the techniques that used to puzzle me became automatic second nature. Buoyed by my increasing skills, I even made a couple of shirts and boxer shorts for my husband.

One day, however, my daughter refused to wear a dress I made her. "It makes me look fat," she told me. She glared defiantly at me with her big eyes in her little six-year-old body. I stood there clutching the dress, shocked. I realized that I must have been putting myself down unwittingly. I mean, where else would a kid learn something like that? How strange to hear my words echoed in a child! Right then and there, I vowed *never* to say anything negative about my body again. It was time to reexamine my relationship with myself.

My mind drifted back to the words: *Sewing completely changes your relationship with your body.* Was it possible for me? Could sewing mend *me*, and this mind that's so willing to tear myself apart?

I often think of how "ease" is a fundamental part of the sewing lingo. There's basic wearing ease, which is the extra amount of fabric added to the garment so you can do human things like breathing and bending down to feed your pet. Then there's style ease that refers to the extra inches added for aesthetic reasons—the loose, flowy Japanese garb that easily doubles as maternity wear is a good example of style ease. I love these kinds of roomy outfits that allow me to breathe and relax. I intuited that sewing may provide an existential ease for me as well—a centering, and a way to reconnect to a quieter, wiser, more creative part of me.

The main reason I avoided sewing for myself boiled down to this: I didn't want to know my actual body measurements. Similar to stepping on the scale, the act of wrapping a measuring tape around my limbs seemed masochistic and unnecessarily cruel. It also seemed difficult to do on my own, and asking anyone else was out of the question. Too embarrassing! But without knowing my own measurements, there was no way of making something that truly fit me.

In fact, when I finally mustered the courage to try sewing for myself, I couldn't even get my arm to fit through the armhole of that first dress. I was still scared of measuring myself and was guesstimating everything. Something had gone terribly, terribly wrong. What's also confusing is that American pattern sizing is usually much larger than ready-to-wear (RTW) sizing. A size 10 in RTW may be a 14 in commercial sewing patterns.

I began examining the meanings that I gave the numbers. If the same size is a 10 in RTW and 14 in sewing patterns, the number must be arbitrary. A size 13 in Japan is extra large, but in the US, the equivalent would be a medium. Even among RTW brands, sizing can vary greatly. Disconcertingly, vanity sizing has been getting smaller and smaller over the years. This means that if you had sauntered into a department store in the '60s and purchased a size 12 dress, and if that exact same dress time traveled to the twenty-first century, it would suddenly be a size 6. *It's all made up.* Despite the willy-nillyness of these numbers, I had swallowed the gospel of "smaller is better." (Exhibit A: the two-sizes-too-small pants that I bought, which nearly suffocated me.) I had lived my life as an active member in the cult of fitting in, trying to squeeze into ill-becoming clothes (and jobs and relationships) because I didn't want to look at who I really was. It was torturous.

Then one random day on which I wasn't even planning on taking my measurements, I reached for the measuring tape, a notebook, and a pen. I'd stitched up a few items for myself here and there, but I was continuing to have trouble determining which size to sew. It turns out that though sewing for yourself can result in a better fit, every pattern requires some sort of alteration. The logical solution was to know the actual dimensions of my body. And I had this hopeful thought: *Would I be able to draft clothes from scratch to fit me and completely bypass altering sewing patterns?* I took a deep, bracing breath. "It's okay, it's okay, it's okay," I repeated silently. I wrapped the measuring tape around my chest, peered down, and recorded the number. Huh. Bigger than I'd hoped. "It's okay, it's okay, it's okay." I moved down to my waist. Whoa. *Way* bigger than I expected! "It's okay." Hips next. Exactly the same as my chest—who knew? I was more cylinder-shaped than hourglass, but this was informative. Thighs, calves, ankles, biceps, torso length, and on and on and on. The numbers crowded the notebook page, and after a while, they stopped looking like judgments.

I put the pen down and sighed. I was ready.

ıılıııılıılıılıılıılıılıılıılıılıılıılıı

I have kept my vow to never to say anything negative about my body out loud. I didn't want my daughter to grow up hearing me put myself down, and I was especially terrified that I might instill an obsession with dieting and self-loathing. Kids have a sixth sense about untruths, though, and they can spot a faker a mile away. I had to learn how to love myself exactly as I was.

I practiced, first and foremost, not saying horrible things about myself out loud. I also knew I had to practice being nice to myself internally. This wasn't something that I was going to do once and be done with. This was going to have to be a lifelong commitment.

This commitment shows up in different ways. I've been a journal writer for over thirty years now, and every day I write down all the things I like about myself, all the things I'm grateful for. I even practice saying loving things to myself in my head. In the past, I have been especially critical about my legs, possibly because my straight-shooting parents would often tell me I had "daikon-ashi" which translates to "radish legs." If you've ever seen a Japanese daikon radish, you'll understand what my legs look like. So I bemoaned my fulsome shanks and avoided wearing shorts and skirts like the plague for *decades*. Now, though, if I happen to look down and see my legs, I find myself thinking, *They're so adorable!* Funnily enough, these days my husband and daughter will also tell me that my legs are cute, apropos of nothing.

As a way to connect to myself, I like to take long walks and allow my mind to wander. This time with and for myself is sacred, and I stay curious in getting to know my feelings, my assumptions, and my knee-jerk reactions. Gently, gently, I let go of the ones that don't seem to work and concentrate on thoughts and feelings and reactions that feel more loving, always tweaking and experimenting. More and more, I notice that the running monologue in the back of my brain is humane and affirming. It's not an effusive cheerleader urging me to win, but more like a wizened grandma simply enjoying my presence without expecting anything of me.

And sewing is another way I commit to self-nurturing. What started out as an outlet for creativity has turned into a unique training ground for accepting and appreciating my body in the here and now. I've learned that creating a well-fitting piece of clothing is not vain or shallow, but a radical act of self-love. I feel so powerful knowing that I'm not beholden to the trends of fashion or mass production. I create what I love exactly how I want to: slowly, sustainably, consciously.

When I catch a glimpse of myself in the mirror these days, I am genuinely and quietly pleased. I don't expect to look like the models in the

'80s-era magazines. I am in my fifties, after all, and I believe I'm evolving in my own lovely way.

Gravity has pressed more firmly upon me. Wrinkles have settled in all over, taking root. My hair is streaked with more and more silver every day. It's simply part of life, I realized. I get to acknowledge that yes, this is my body and hey, it's downright incredible. Like my college friend Shelly from so long ago, I'm learning how to like myself no matter what. To love myself, even. It's never too late, and it's a beautiful thing.

When we are young, fitting in matters so much. And as time softens our expectations and deepens our experiences, opening our eyes to how little we actually know of what's going on, we start to fit into the universe exactly as ourselves. I've given up my fruitless search for the outfit some-where *out there* that would help me fit in the world. I'm exactly who and where I'm supposed to be, and I create clothes (and everything else) from that state of being.

Sometimes, I like to browse through retail stores. I meander and touch the clothes, admiring the fabric texture, examining the hem, and how the seams are finished. I never buy anything, but I leave with a brain full of ideas and inspiration. It's remarkable to me that when I walk into a cloth-ing store now, I am confident that I can make anything and everything on the racks, but in exactly the way *I* want to. So empowering! This is one of the greatest gifts of sewing: creating for who you really are. But that starts with understanding ourselves, examining our deeply held beliefs, and being willing to be a little uncomfortable. Without a doubt, an abundance of one-of-a-kind, delightful clothes can be stitched up through persisting and enjoying and steeping ourselves in the process all the way. It will seem like magic. It is definitely about sewing love, and really, that's the best kind of enchantment.

Lookbook

LEFT: TANK TOP (PAGE 125)
AND ELASTIC-WAISTED
SHORTS WITH SLASH
POCKETS (PAGE 193)

RIGHT: KNIT CAP SLEEVE
DRESS (PAGE 165)

RACERBACK TANK DRESS (PAGE 171)
AND SLEEVELESS DRESS WITH
POCKETS (PAGE 157)

LEFT: V-NECK SLEEVELESS DRESS (PAGE 163)
AND CARDIGAN WITH CURVED HEM (PAGE 239)

RIGHT: BATEAU TOP (PAGE 149) AND
BACK ZIP A-LINE SKIRT (PAGE 223)

LEFT: V-NECK TOP (PAGE 140) AND
WIDE-LEG PANTS WITH FLAT-FRONT
WAISTBAND + ELASTIC BACK (PAGE 203)

RIGHT: BUTTON-DOWN V-NECK TOP
(PAGE 146) AND DRAWSTRING-
WAISTBAND SHORTS (PAGE 200)

LEFT: BATEAU TOP (PAGE 149) AND
WIDE-LEG PANTS WITH FLAT-FRONT
WAISTBAND + ELASTIC BACK (PAGE 203)

RIGHT: LONG SLEEVE TEE WITH CUFFS
(PAGE 138) AND SKIRT WITH INVERTED
BOX PLEAT (PAGE 231)

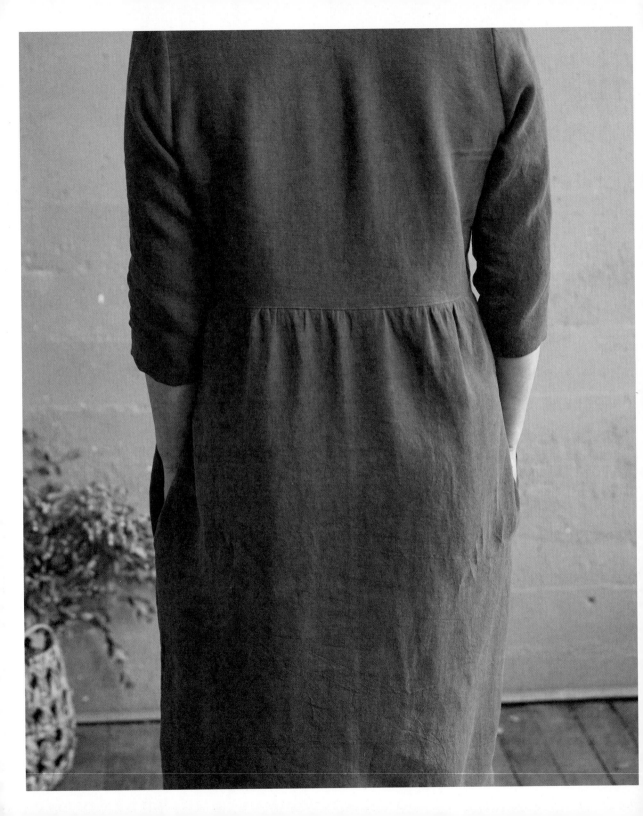

BANDED COLLAR DRESS WITH
POCKETS (PAGE 182)

LEFT: KNIT COCOON TUNIC DRESS
(PAGE 175) AND LEGGINGS (PAGE 220)

RIGHT: BATWING TOP (PAGE 181)
AND LEGGINGS (PAGE 220)

LEFT: FLARED COAT (PAGE 257) OVER WOVEN TEE (PAGE 155) AND STRAIGHT-LEG PANTS WITH CURVED POCKETS (PAGE 210)

RIGHT: DRAPEY JACKET WITH POCKETS (PAGE 240) OVER TANK TOP (PAGE 125) AND WIDE-LEG PANTS WITH FLAT-FRONT WAISTBAND + ELASTIC BACK (PAGE 203)

LEFT: CARDIGAN (PAGE 233) OVER TANK
TOP (PAGE 125)

RIGHT: HANTEN COAT (PAGE 249) OVER
WOVEN TEE (PAGE 155) AND SLIM-FIT
SIDE ZIP PANTS (PAGE 213)

BUTTON-DOWN TUNIC (PAGE 190) AND
SLIM-FIT SIDE ZIP PANTS (PAGE 213)

LEFT: T-SHIRT (PAGE 133) AND STRAIGHT-LEG PANTS WITH CURVED POCKETS (PAGE 210)

RIGHT: MINIMALIST DRAPEY JACKET (PAGE 247) OVER KNIT CAP SLEEVE DRESS (PAGE 165)

the
foundation

Sewing Basics

The art and science of sewing is full of techniques. Here I've listed a few recommendations for tools and materials that I feel will be most helpful in creating the projects in this book, along with a quick overview of nice-to-know stitching tips and tricks.

SEWING TOOLS

BODKINS/SAFETY PINS: A bodkin is used to thread elastic through casings; some look and work like tweezers, but there are many styles. No bodkin? No problem. A safety pin is just as effective. Simply secure one end of the elastic on the bodkin or through the safety pin needle, and thread through the casing, making sure that the unsecured end doesn't get lost in the casing.

HAND-SEWING NEEDLES: There are a bunch of hand-sewing needles available, so you might want to test out a few to find your preference.

PINCUSHION/MAGNETIC PIN HOLDER: To corral loose pins, it's a good idea to keep them contained in an easily accessible way. The classic pincushion is a good choice, but my go-to is a magnetic pin holder.

RULERS: Various rulers come in handy when drafting slopers and garments. Several are mentioned in this book, including the gridded quilting ruler (see cutting tools on the following page), a French curve, a hip curve, and a styling design ruler. The last three are pretty much interchangeable, so you need only one of them. My favorite is the styling design ruler, but the French curve is a close second.

SEAM RIPPER: A vital tool.

SEWING CLIPS A.K.A. WONDER CLIPS: These are more of a bonus supply. These clips serve as an alternative to pins to hold pieces together while you sew and are useful for temporarily securing zippers as well.

SEWING MACHINE(S): Any standard sewing machine will do. Although I also reference a serger or overlocker for projects that use stretchy fabric, you really only need a sewing machine with a zigzag stitch. If you have a serger or overlocker, by all means feel free to use it, as it's quite a time-saver.

SEWING MACHINE FEET: Most of the projects can be completed with your standard presser foot. There are several project variations that require a buttonhole foot (Button-Down V-Neck Top, page 146; Button-Down Tunic, page 190; and Drawstring-Waistband Shorts, page 200) and two projects that would benefit from both a regular and an invisible zipper foot (Slim-Fit Side Zip Pants, page 213, and Back Zip A-Line Skirt, page 223).

SEWING MACHINE NEEDLES: I recommend having two types of needles on hand—all-purpose and knit-friendly needles. Knit-friendly needles are typically labeled "ballpoint," "stretch," or "jersey," and any one of those will do.

SMALL SCISSORS: These are handy for snipping all the threads as you sew and easier to use than a regular pair of scissors when clipping curves and corners of seam allowances.

STRAIGHT PINS: My favorites are cellulose tulip-headed pins made by Hiroshima Needles for quilting and pinning fine fabrics. However, any kind of pin is great.

THREAD: The all-purpose polyester variety works just fine for all the projects.

CUTTING TOOLS

I can't stress the importance of "measure twice and cut once" enough. I have pulled out many a hair after failing to double-check my measurements.

CUTTING MAT: Look for these self-healing mats in the largest size you can afford because they will become indispensable. Not only are they essential when using your rotary cutter, but the ruled grid also makes measuring fabric a cinch. The cutting mat surface also keeps the fabric from shifting around.

FABRIC SHEARS: A pair of bent-handle fabric shears is well worth the investment.

GRIDDED QUILTING RULER: You've probably seen these see-through rulers around. An 18-inch quilting ruler is great for drafting patterns, marking lines, and using the rotary cutter. A 24-inch ruler is even lovelier and probably more effective for garment sewing.

MARKING TOOLS: There are so many marking tools available, and some of my favorites include ones with disappearing ink (some disappear on their own, while others disappear when you spray water on or iron the fabric) and the Chaco Liner Pen Style chalk marker, which makes very precise markings. You will need a marking tool for every project in this book.

PATTERN WEIGHTS: Metal washers of varying sizes make great pattern weights. They work fabulously for holding pattern pieces in place on fabric as you trace around them. Use them individually or stacked (the slipperier the fabric, the more weights I use).

ROTARY CUTTER: The razor-sharp, rotating blades are especially ideal for cutting straight lines along the edge of a ruler on a cutting mat. Nowadays there are models with smaller blades that better accommodate cutting around curves.

PRESSING TOOLS

A proper ironing—or "pressing" in sewing lingo—can make a massive difference in the outcome of a project. Pressing isn't simply for smoothing out wrinkles; it also ensures accurate stitching and reinforces the shape of a sewn item.

IRON: A basic model that has a steam option and a few heat settings is more than enough. Keep in mind that you are, in fact, pressing with the iron and not gliding it back and forth over the fabric. Firmly place your iron in the desired spot, hold for a few seconds, then slide to an adjacent spot and hold again.

IRONING BOARD: I use a traditional ironing board, though any tabletop or flat surface will quickly convert to an ironing board with a thick, heat-resistant mat on top. You could even build your own customized ironing station with some plywood, batting, and heat-resistant fabric.

SEAM GAUGE: These small metal rulers are used to measure hems and folded edges of fabric. They usually include a slot with a little plastic slider to help you create various seam allowances too. A small ruler will do the job as well.

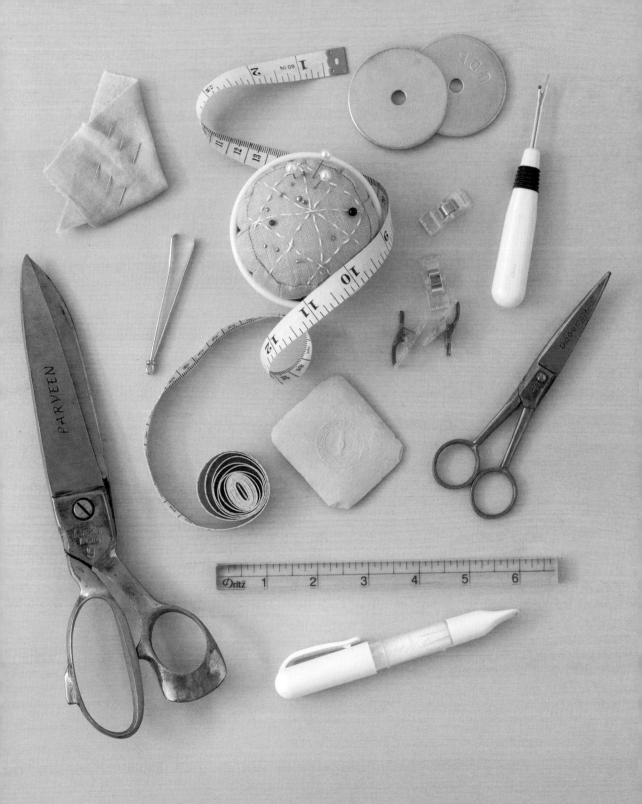

THE DRAFTING KIT

All of the projects in this book call for the "drafting kit," which is my fancy way of saying you'll need some paper, a ruler, and a writing utensil to draw your own pattern pieces. For specific tools, terminologies, and techniques, see page 65.

RECOMMENDED FABRICS

One of the best parts of sewing is the creative freedom to combine a pattern with a fabric of your choice. The same project can look entirely different depending on the fabric you use, and the options are infinite. See page 262 for fabric guide resources. Here's a list of my most frequently recommended fabrics:

COTTON: Easy to sew, plentifully available, and infinite in variety, it's pretty hard to go wrong with cotton. This all-purpose fabric will work well for most of the projects in this book, though you will want to avoid using quilting cotton for garments in general.

DOUBLE GAUZE: I love to use light and airy double gauze for warm-weather tops and dresses.

KNITS/STRETCH FABRICS: The main differentiator between wovens (such as linen, cotton, and double gauze) and knits is that knit fabrics stretch. Knits can range in drape, weight, texture, and substrate content like all fabrics, but their versatility is second to none. Bonus: the edges don't fray in most knits. Using a zigzag stitch and sewing machine needles designed for stretch fabrics (see page 133) is highly recommended, especially if you don't own a serger.

LINEN: I just can't get enough of this beautifully textured fabric woven from the fibers of the flax plant.

RAYON: Although it is a human-made fiber, rayon isn't synthetic and is derived from wood pulp. The thin fibers allow this textile to breathe, and it's a lovely fabric for drapey, summery tops and dresses.

WOOL: The vast array of wool fabric available can leave your head spinning, but I like to stick with wool crepe (lightweight crepe is especially nice), wool jersey, tweed, and flannel. These are the easiest to sew and hide many sewing errors.

HANDY TERMS + TECHNIQUES

Sewing can often feel overwhelming with the zillions of stitches and techniques available. In this section, I've rounded up the basics. The following isn't intended to be a comprehensive guide to sewing but a highlight reel of things to keep in mind as you start on the projects. For more intensive sewing instruction, check out the books listed in Resources on page 262.

ALIGNING: A necessary step in pattern drafting that ensures all the pattern pieces align properly. Truing up and walking are related to this process, and I use the term "align" to include both. See page 67 for more details.

BACKSTITCHING: Though it's usually not called out in the projects, you will be backstitching at the start and end of each seam. This means that you will sew a few stitches, then select your back button (or pull or lever or whatever functionality for reversing that your machine is equipped with) to sew backward over the first few stitches you created (or the last few if you are indeed at the end). I normally backstitch four or five stitches, and you can consider this step the equivalent of tying a knot to secure it. Otherwise, your stitches will unravel and your hard work will be for naught.

BASTE: A basting stitch holds pieces of fabric together temporarily. This can be done on the machine with a lengthened stitch or by hand with a running stitch.

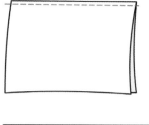

BIAS TAPE: My favorite way to encase or bind raw edges at the neckline and armholes is with bias tape. Strips of fabric are cut on the bias (see page 48), which gives the fabric stretchiness, even if it's not a knit fabric. You'll notice that sometimes I call them facings and sometimes bindings. In general, if the bias tape is on the underside of the garment and not visible, it's considered a facing. If it's visible, or sandwiches a seam allowance, it's often called a binding.

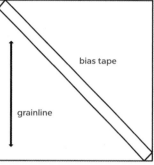

bias tape

grainline

CLIPPING: When sewing curves, I will instruct you to clip into the seam allowance without cutting into the seamline. This is to prevent puckering in sections like curved pockets and necklines.

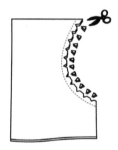

EDGESTITCH: This type of stitching is at the very edge of the fold of a fabric, usually ⅛ inch or less from the edge. It is often meant to be decorative, but in my projects, edgestitching is more often utilized as reinforcement or to close up openings from which pieces are turned right side out. Edgestitching is also used for finishing hems. Traditionally, topstitching (see page 51) is the preferred method for finishing hems, but my sewing machine has very even tension for stitches on both sides, so edgestitching works well. If your stitches look less uniform on the underside (the bobbin side), you may want to use topstitching to finish your hems instead, unless you don't mind the imperfect look.

FABRIC PREPARATION: Make sure to prewash and dry all fabrics. You will also want to iron/press the fabric before you begin drafting or tracing patterns onto it. The exception to this general rule is wool fabric. You can actually toss most wool fabrics into a washing machine for a short cycle with cold water, but don't use a dryer, as it will become fulled or felted. Air dry instead.

FINISHING: Fabrics such as cotton and linen will fray, so to prevent fabric edges from unraveling and turning into an unwieldy mass of threads, they need to be "finished." This can be done in several ways, such as by zigzag stitching or by overlock stitching if you have a serger/overlocker. Some textiles recommended in this book will not fray, including knits and some wool fabrics, so finishing the raw edges is optional.

GRAINLINE: The grainline will guide you when cutting out pattern pieces from fabric. The straight grain is parallel to the selvage (see page 50). The cross grain is perpendicular (at a right angle) to the straight grain. And cutting on the bias means cutting diagonally, at a 45-degree angle. Think of it as a tic-tac-toe grid. The vertical lines are straight grain, the horizontal lines are cross grain, and if you get three Xs in a diagonal row, it's a bias grain. The pattern pieces are marked with straight grain lines when appropriate.

I determine the grainline by what I call the "pull test." I tug at a piece of fabric to see which way it stretches more. If I pull up and down and it stretches more than it does from side to side, then I know that the selvage edge is at one of the sides, and the grainline is running up and down. And vice versa. So the direction that the fabric stretches *less* is parallel to the selvage.

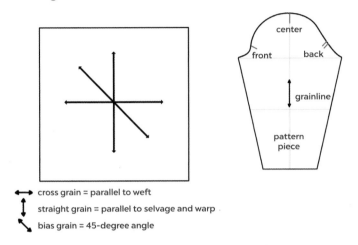

↔ cross grain = parallel to weft

↕ straight grain = parallel to selvage and warp

↘ bias grain = 45-degree angle

MARKINGS: When you draft your garments, it's a good idea to add markings onto your paper patterns to indicate which piece is the front/back, where pockets are positioned, etc. These markings will then be transferred to the fabric via notches cut into the fabric or chalk marks. The markings help avoid confusion during the construction steps. I like to mark back pieces/sections with 2 notches and other sections with one notch.

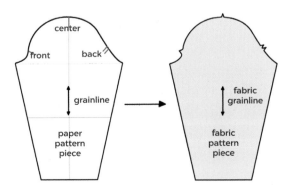

ON THE FOLD: When tracing pattern pieces onto fabric, sometimes you will need to place the pattern piece "on the fold" of the fabric to cut out symmetrical pieces, such as the front bodice of a tank top. Make sure to fold the fabric with the grainline running vertically and place the center section of the pattern piece (also known as the center fold line) flush against the fold.

RIGHT SIDE/WRONG SIDE: The "right side" (RS) refers to the outer-facing side of the fabric, and the "wrong side" (WS) is the interior-facing side of the fabric. Sometimes it's pretty obvious, but there are times when a fabric looks identical on both sides. In such cases, I recommend using your marking tool to indicate the wrong side to make assembling the pieces easier down the line.

SEAM ALLOWANCE: The seam allowance is the section of fabric between the stitching line and the edge of the fabric when at least two pieces of material are sewn together. The seam allowance will vary across and within each project, so I've made sure to include specific seam allowance information in each step. It is phrased as "sew ⅛ inch from the raw edge" or as "sew with a ⅛-inch seam allowance."

SELVAGE: Selvage is the nonfraying edge of a piece of fabric that runs parallel to what's called the warp. When you buy fabric, it's the section of the fabric with the brand and designer information printed on a thin strip along one edge. The warp comprises threads that run longitudinally—in other words, vertically or up and down—and the weft comprises the threads that are woven in and out between the warp threads. See the illustration for Grainline (page 49).

SLIP STITCH: Some of the projects reference slip-stitching by hand to close openings in a seam. You will start by double knotting the end of your thread and inserting your needle from the underside of one opening edge to hide the knot. Pull the needle all the way through and pick up a few threads in the fabric directly across from where you pulled out your needle. Then pick up a few threads from the other side, inserting the needle from under the seam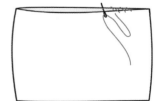

slightly away from the original stitch. Continue stitching this way until the opening is closed. Knot the thread, then insert the needle and pull out about ½ inch from the insertion point to hide the knot. Clip the thread.

STAYSTITCH: Since necklines are typically cut into a curve, the fabric has a tendency to stretch. This could result in wonky necklines, and a way to prevent this is to stitch within the seam allowance along the neckline before assembling the pieces together. I usually stitch about ¼ inch from the edge.

STITCH IN THE DITCH: This is a technique that I reference quite a bit in attaching waistbands. You will be sewing through the seam, from the right side of the seam that joins the waistband and shorts, pants, or skirt, to catch the facing on the other side. Think of the joining seam as the "ditch," hence the name. Pinning the facing at the seam helps guide you in stitching in the ditch. Go slowly, since it's easy to miss stitching the facing.

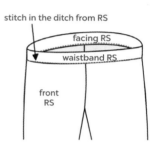

stitch in the ditch from RS

facing RS

waistband RS

front RS

SQUARING CORNERS: To prevent odd pointy bits where pattern pieces are joined, it's important to "square the corner." This means that sections of a pattern piece that form a corner should be at a right angle. See page 72 for more details.

TOPSTITCH: Decorative or functional, topstitching is a line of stitching sewn from the right side of the fabric.

TRIMMING: The term used for cutting seam allowances down.

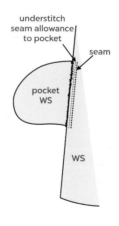

understitch seam allowance to pocket

seam

pocket WS

WS

UNDERSTITCHING: Most often used for securing linings, facings, and pocket linings, understitching is sewing a line close to the edge of a facing or lining to join it to the seam allowance. This secures the lining or facing in a way that prevents it from rolling toward the outside.

Slopers + Muslins: The Secret to Lovely Fit

"Wait!" you may be wondering. "What's a *sloper*?"

Slopers, also called blocks, are the foundational paper pattern pieces created from your unique body measurements. I like to think of them as 2-D dress forms made exactly for you. These are no-frills, absolutely basic pattern pieces from which all other pattern pieces can be designed. After you make your slopers, you'll make muslins, which are the fabric versions of your slopers, and you'll get an opportunity to test and tweak further when you make the muslins.

Okay, first things first: all you perfectionists, I see you. I feel you. I'm a recovering perfectionist myself, and I know that the temptation will be to work on these slopers until the fit is absolutely spot on. Don't do it. Trust me on this—I made five versions of the lower body sloper until I finally realized that the weird wrinkle I just couldn't eliminate near my left butt cheek wasn't going to make any difference in the fit of the finished garment.

Now, don't let slopers intimidate you. The idea of creating a sloper was daunting for me at first, and I assumed that it would take me months to get it right. Although it did take me a few tries over the course of several days to get a fit that I liked, the process isn't difficult at all. And when I say "a few tries over the course of several days," the actual total number of hours was less than five per sloper. Like anything, you could get lost in the fine-tuning and could possibly fiddle with the slopers for months (or even years), but we're striving for "good enough for now." What you gain from these few hours is invaluable knowledge of your true body shape and a starting point that guarantees a fit better than any ready-to-wear garment out there. And here's a tidbit if you didn't already know: *all* the commercial patterns and garments out in the big wide world begin as a sloper. The thing is, the sloper in question is based on someone else's body (or an imaginary, ideal body), so unless you happen to be an exact body double to whomever was the basis of the sloper, nothing out there is ever going to perfectly fit *you*.

A lovely fit looks different for everyone, and no two slopers will be identical. In fact, during the testing phase for this book, it was remarkable and inspiring to see the diverse shapes of the slopers my testers made. None of us come out of the womb shaped symmetrically, and age just amplifies all the variations in our bodies. In many cases we'll need to account for uneven measurements for particular anatomical sections. For example, I have a right calf that is almost a half-inch bigger than my left calf, my breasts are lopsided, and my left shoulder juts out farther than my right, which is higher than my left. This is why ease—the extra inches added to pattern pieces—plays a vital role. Ease allows us to move in our clothes and takes natural bodily asymmetry into consideration.

Remember, the goal here is "good enough," and the time you save by not going down the rabbit hole of the "perfect" sloper will be much better spent on refining the actual garments you'll be making based off of the slopers, because if you've ever sewn the same pattern in different fabrics, you know that the fit and result are always slightly different. As Barbara Emodi says in her excellent book, *SEW . . . The Garment-Making Book of Knowledge*, "we're building a skirt, not a rocket." Let's not take the process too seriously, and you'll enjoy it so much more. And to quote another sewing luminary, "Anyone who can work through the labyrinthian directions for sewing that accompany the commercial pattern can surely learn the comparatively simple and clear rules for pattern-making." Preach it, Adele P. Margolis.

As you start to create your slopers, please keep in mind two important things.

First, this is not meant to be a be-all and end-all set of instructions for slopers and fit issues, but rather my tried-and-tested method to create basic pieces that will allow you to easily draft the projects featured in this book. You could also use patterns you already own or a well-fitting top (with sleeves) and pants to draft the projects instead. And for those of you interested in diving deeper into the fine art of sloper creation and fitting, check out the Resources on page 262.

Second, creating a sloper is *not* about judging your body. This is about understanding and accepting your amazing human shape just as it is. It's truly the most essential part. You'll get to familiarize yourself with what feels right for YOU, with the body you have right now. It involves paying very close attention as well as loads and loads of open-mindedness and compassion. I can't even tell you how empowering it is to know how to fit my unique body from scratch instead of trying to alter existing patterns. Numbers will become effective tools and not some sort of punitive scorecard. At the same time, having these slopers will definitely aid you in adjusting any commercial pattern you may already have in your stash or will be adding in the future, though I won't be covering that in this book. (For information on adjusting commercial patterns, check out the Resources on page 262.) Consider this a starting point. Ultimately, with some patience and some practice, by creating your own slopers you'll be able to make silhouettes that embrace your body beautifully and are fully expressive of you—what's available on the market won't even come close. It's been a *huge* game changer for me.

Ready?

Alright, let's dive in.

So what kind of slopers are we making? We are going to create three foundation pieces based on your measurements:

THE TORSO SLOPER

Most slopers have darts because we are three-dimensional beings and darts help create the concave and convex curves that make up the contours of our bodies. However, since most of the projects in this book will have plenty of ease, I've opted to simplify the torso sloper into a dartless version with an option to add a dart or simply add extra inches around the bust instead. Depending on your dimensions, you may need to add extra length to the hem since the larger the bust, the more the fabric will lift up. I rarely wear tops and dresses with darts, and the ones featured in this book are dartless (except for one), so I wanted to be consistent in the sloper phase as well. If, however, you'd like to add darts to provide extra shaping for all the tops and dresses you'll make, I've included that option. But in my experience (and I've been told my chest is quite big for my frame), the dartless version works just fine. We'll be drafting a front piece and a back piece for the torso sloper.

THE SLEEVE SLOPER

Sleeves can seem tricky given the curvatures involved with the sleeve cap, which is the bell-shaped part of the sleeve at the top. There are whole volumes devoted to discussing high, medium, and low sleeve caps and the inscrutable armscye (or armhole) to cap formula. But numerous sources agree that the actual curve of the sleeve cap is rather inconsequential as long as the curve length of the sleeve cap matches the armhole to which you're attaching the sleeve. The sleeve cap curve can even be up to an inch larger than the armhole and still fit well! After much experimentation, I've found this to be true. As with everything else in sewing, it boils down to preference and tinkering and making lots of mistakes. You'll be surprised at how easy it is to actually draft the sleeve sloper. The fun part is figuring out what kind of sleeve fit feels right for you.

THE LOWER BODY SLOPER

We're going to multi-purpose the lower body sloper (a.k.a. the pants sloper) for all lower body patterns: shorts, skirts, and pants. I have no waist or derriere to speak of and my stomach is on the flatter side, so I've found darts unnecessary; however, many folks will want to add darts to the lower body sloper, so I've included a quick way of doing that (for more details on darts, see the section on page 69). I've noticed that there's so much fear-mongering when it comes to drafting and sewing pants, but with the will to learn and a bit of patience, it's *totally* doable. I've worked hard to simplify the process, and for me, the lower body sloper actually took less time to adjust for a decent fit than the torso sloper. If you've ever hunted for well-fitting jeans and experienced the agony of the fruitless chase, you'll find that creating this sloper is the holy grail. You'll never look back, trust me.

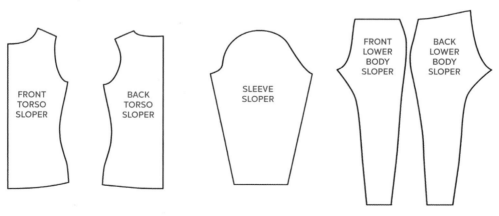

A WORD ON MUSLINS AND FIT

Once the initial slopers have been drafted, you'll be sewing up a *muslin* (sometimes called a *toile*) to test the fit. A sloper is your initial pattern piece made with paper, and a muslin is the fabric version. This phase is the magic sauce. I highly recommend using old sheets or any inexpensive cotton fabrics you may have in your stash to sew the muslins. Try to use fabric with a tight weave; linen tends to be loosely woven, and knits are designed to expand, so both will stretch out too much to give you a proper fit assessment. There's also actual white or off-white muslin fabric that you can use, available at most fabric stores. Light, solid colors allow for easy-to-see markings, which you will transfer to your paper slopers as you make adjustments. Use basting stitches, don't bother finishing raw edges, and keep your seam ripper handy.

In terms of fitting adjustments, there are four main ones you'll be making: lengthening or shortening and widening or narrowing.

These four manipulations will affect each other, of course, and there is a conventional rule of thumb to the order of modifications, which is to first lengthen or shorten; second, widen or narrow; and third, make any other modifications. But don't get too hung up on this order, as you'll start to develop a sense of what alterations will work best.

TRANSFERRING MARKINGS

When you sew up a muslin to test the fit of your slopers, you will inevitably make modifications. The easiest way for me to transfer markings is to first draw directly on the muslin fabric, then transfer the marks to the paper sloper pattern. For example, if my muslin is gaping open, I will pinch the excess fabric as if I'm creating a dart, and draw lines along the base of the pinched fabric. Since I use Swedish tracing paper for pattern drafting (see page 66), I place the sloper pattern on top of the muslin and trace the amount of fabric that I need to remove. I usually pinch the same amount on the sloper and tape it down like a dart, or sometimes I will cut a slit and overlap or spread the section to match the muslin adjustment (see Tightening on page 60).

Most of the time you can directly transfer your markings from muslin to sloper. The notable exception is the neckline because you don't want to affect the center part of the neckline curve (see Squaring Corners, page 72). If you have to increase or decrease a portion of the neckline, divide the measurement by half (the sloper is designed to represent half of your body and will be cut on the fold [see page 50]) and make the modifications a little off-center.

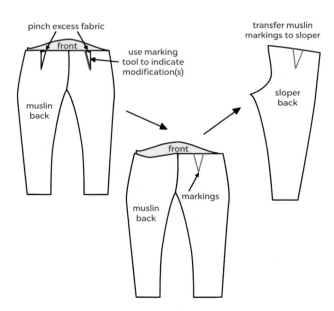

Conversely, if a section is too tight, let's say at the armhole, I will mark where I see or feel tightness on the muslin, then I add extra width to the sloper at the same spot by cutting a slit, spreading it the appropriate amount, and securing additional tracing paper with tape to the section to replace the missing paper. On the torso, the armhole is the most common tight spot.

There's a bit of guesswork involved with every adjustment, and it's always a good idea to err on the conservative side. Once I've made changes to the sloper pattern pieces, I like to cut out and sew another muslin. Those with extra analytical or methodical minds tend to create a new sloper pattern for every single modification as well as a separate muslin for each change, but I prefer to identify all the adjustments I can find with each muslin fitting, transfer them to the sloper pattern pieces (they start to resemble Frankenstein with all the additional pieces of paper and tape), then sew a new muslin. Whatever works for you. Once I have a decent fit, I trace the sloper pattern pieces onto durable tagboard. Remember our motto: "good enough for now!"

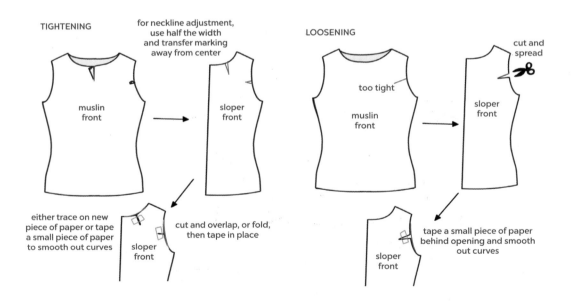

TIGHTENING

for neckline adjustment, use half the width and transfer marking away from center

LOOSENING

cut and spread

muslin front

sloper front

too tight

muslin front

sloper front

either trace on new piece of paper or tape a small piece of paper to smooth out curves

sloper front

cut and overlap, or fold, then tape in place

sloper front

tape a small piece of paper behind opening and smooth out curves

Because the sloper muslins closely fit the body, I leave one side either partially or entirely unsewn for the torso and lower body pieces so I can slip them on and off easily to check the fit (I pin or hold the unsewn side). Another option is to cut a slit along the center front from the waistline to just below the armhole measurement. Some folks like to cut the back in half at the center and add a zipper, but that's up to you.

TORSO MUSLIN GOALS: For the torso muslin, the aim is for the neckline to lay as flat as possible and the armhole to have little to no gaping open at the front and back, while still allowing you to lift your arms. The shoulder seam should be centered along the top of your shoulder and the outer edge will be at the joint where the shoulder and arm meet. You may see a few wrinkles and puckers around the bust, which is normal since we're not including darts. We also want the hem to be level across the front and back.

SLEEVE MUSLIN GOALS: You want the sleeve muslin to fit nicely into the armhole and for it to hang from the shoulder down to the wrist without twisting. Marking the grainline on the muslin pieces may help to assess twisting issues. A good sleeve fit is when the wrinkles and puckers are

TORSO MUSLIN GOALS

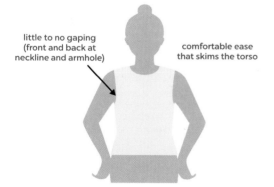

little to no gaping
(front and back at
neckline and armhole)

comfortable ease
that skims the torso

SLEEVE MUSLIN GOALS

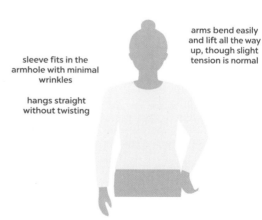

sleeve fits in the
armhole with minimal
wrinkles

hangs straight
without twisting

arms bend easily
and lift all the way
up, though slight
tension is normal

minimal (you will never be able to eliminate all wrinkles and puckers; I've tried and it's impossible) and you can easily lift your arms without excessive tightness at the front or back. Since it's a fairly close-fitting sleeve, you may find there's some tension when you lift your arm all the way up, and this is normal.

LOWER BODY MUSLIN GOALS: For the lower body muslin, waist-to-hip and the crotch or rise area are often the focal points for fit. Depending on how curvy your figure is, you may want to experiment a little or a lot with dart depth and placement. A well-fitting pants muslin will sit comfortably at your preferred waistline, without feeling too loose or too tight around the stomach, crotch, and hips. The fabric should skim the legs, but the ankle opening will be looser to be large enough for the foot to go through. The fabric will hang with the grain without twisting around the legs.

LOWER MUSLIN GOALS

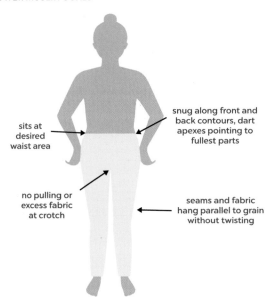

sits at
desired
waist area

snug along front and
back contours, dart
apexes pointing to
fullest parts

no pulling or
excess fabric
at crotch

seams and fabric
hang parallel to grain
without twisting

EVERY BODY IS UNIQUE

As you draft your slopers and garments, remember that there is a wide range of body types and your sloper may not look like the illustrations shown in the instructions. Here are a few examples of slopers—you can see they can look quite different.

Every single body is magnificently, wonderfully distinct.

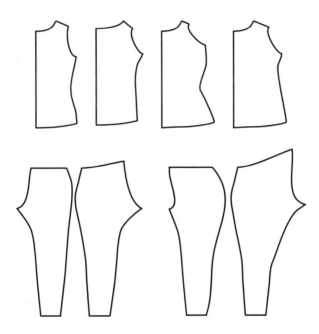

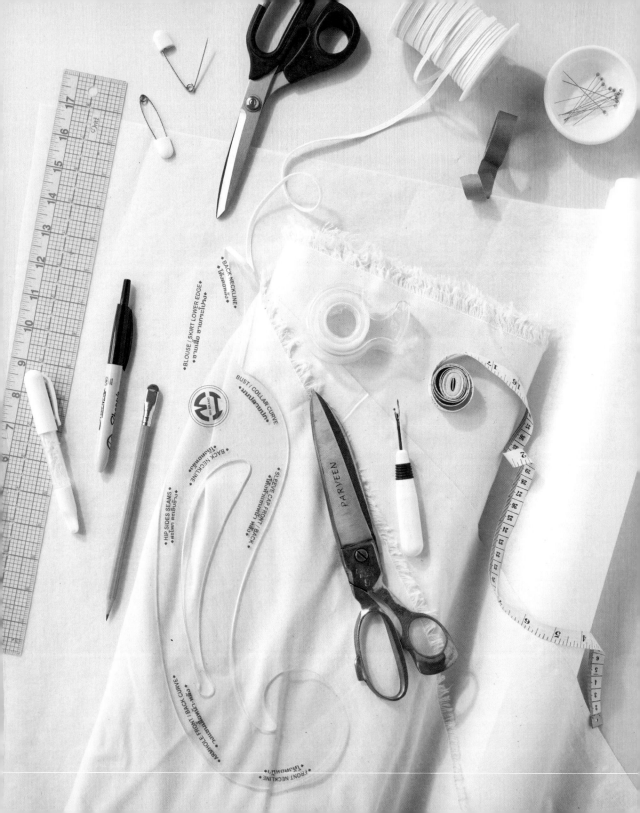

PATTERN DRAFTING OVERVIEW

This section gives you a list of tools and covers some terminology and techniques that may not be familiar to you. It's a good idea to skim through this section before you get started. However, I know that it can feel a little overwhelming to get all this information up front. Since the instructions will refer you back to the appropriate terminologies and techniques, feel free to gather your tools, skip the drafting terms and concepts for now, and go straight to the measurements section.

DRAFTING TOOLS AND SUPPLIES

Here's everything that you need for drafting both the slopers and the garment projects. I've marked items that are specific to creating slopers with an asterisk, meaning you won't need these items to draft the garment projects later in the book.

- Elastic to tie around your waist*
- Mirror (two mirrors is even better, so you can get a good back view)*
- Necklace, chain, or similar item to drape around your neck*
- Sharpie or alternate marking utensil for marking muslins*
- Tape or erasable marker for marking measuring points on your body (Note: you'll place small pieces of tape on your body or base-layer garments. I like to use painter's tape.)*
- Fabric-marking tools such as chalk or erasable markers
- Fabric shears for cutting muslin fabric
- French curve or styling design ruler
- Glue stick or transparent tape
- Measuring tape
- Muslin fabric or any tightly woven cotton fabric that's not precious to you
- Notebook and pen (or your favorite notes app) to record measurements and general information

- Paper for pattern-making (Note: any large pieces of paper will do, but tracing paper makes pattern-making much easier, since all the projects in the book start with tracing the slopers. My favorite is Swedish tracing paper, and Pellon 830 Easy Pattern is a very similar, economical alternative available online and at most retail sewing/ big-box craft stores.)
- Pencil
- Safety pins and straight pins
- Scissors for cutting paper
- Seam ripper (you'll need it, trust me)
- Sewing machine (for basting muslins)
- Transparent gridded quilting ruler, 18 or 24 inches long

Optional (but very helpful):
- Flexible curve ruler
- Hip ruler—an elongated version of the French curve or styling design ruler
- Tagboard (a.k.a. oak tag paper)—once you have slopers and patterns that you like, you might want to copy them onto this durable paper
- Seam gauge
- Yard stick

DRAFTING TERMS AND CONCEPTS

ADDING SEAM ALLOWANCES

A seam allowance is the extra bit of fabric at the edge of a pattern piece between the seam line—the exact place you'll sew the fabric together—and the outside edge of the fabric. Seam allowances will need to be added to your pattern pieces once the drafting is complete. The easiest way to add them is to take a ruler or seam gauge and mark the specified seam allowance amount along the outer edge of the pattern. You can add the seam allowance to the paper pattern prior to tracing it onto fabric (if you've already cut out the paper pattern, you'll need to re-trace it onto a bigger piece of paper to add the seam allowance). Alternatively, you can trace the pattern on the fabric, then add the seam allowance on the fabric itself.

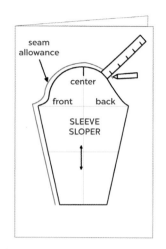

ALIGNING PATTERN PIECES: "TRUING UP" AND "WALKING"

When you create a sloper or garment, you will have multiple pattern pieces. To make sure that the corresponding pattern pieces can be sewn together correctly, they need to be *walked* and/or *trued up*. This is very important! For the purpose of this book, I will refer to this step as "aligning," and you can choose whichever method you like.

Truing up involves measuring seam lines, and *walking* involves physically lining up pattern pieces as if you're sewing them together to verify that corresponding sections are matching up in length or width. Typically, you would check that inner and outer pant leg, shoulder, side, and sleeve-to-armhole seams align.

To walk and/or true up pieces, you will be measuring or lining up the pattern pieces so that the seams, darts, and hems match up *before* adding seam allowances. In

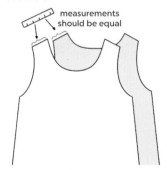

TRUING UP

this book, I recommend roughly cutting out your drafted pieces to walk the seams, since I find it easier to see if the pieces are matching up that way (walking) than by measuring each section (truing up). If you use Swedish tracing paper, you can easily overlap the pieces to do this.

If the pattern pieces don't align, you'll adjust the pattern, making any necessary changes. For example, for the shoulder seam, you have two ways to do it.

(1) True Up: Measure the width of the front and back shoulder pattern pieces to see if they are the same. If they are different, determine which dimension you prefer by laying the pattern piece on your body. Mark and then correct the one that's too long or too short, or split the difference.

(2) Walking: Alternatively, you could walk the front and back shoulders by aligning them and comparing the length, then making adjustments. The term *walking* makes more sense when aligning the side or sleeve-to-the armhole seam, since you have to shift the pattern pieces around each other to see if the lengths and widths match up. Walking the sleeve is probably the least intuitive—fortunately, the sleeve cap can be a little bit bigger than the armhole and still fit well. The term "easing" is used to describe stretching the armhole to fit the slightly bigger sleeve cap, and you'll see it occasionally for other design elements. In the illustrations below, the pink sections need to be aligned.

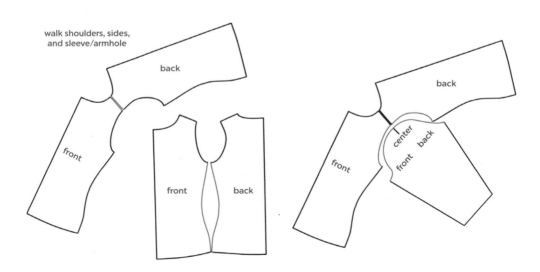

walk shoulders, sides, and sleeve/armhole

back

front

front   back

back

center

front   back

front

DARTS

What is a dart? It's usually a triangular piece of fabric that is folded and sewn to create three-dimensional shaping out of a flat piece of fabric. Most of the time darts are incorporated at the bust or waist, though some patterns also have shoulder, armhole and elbow darts. As someone with a cylindrical body from the rib cage down, I have very little need for darts. Many people, however, like the contouring that darts provide.

A dart is made up of two parts: dart legs and dart apex.

The long and short of it is that you draw a triangle with the pointy end—called the apex—directed at the fullest body part that you're contouring your pattern to fit. If it's your bust, then the dart apex will point toward the bust apex (or nipple). If it's your backside, the dart apex will point toward the fullest part of, well, each cheek. The apex should end about an inch or two before the fullest part. The standard dart length is about 3 to 4 inches, but as always, experiment with this to see what works best for your body.

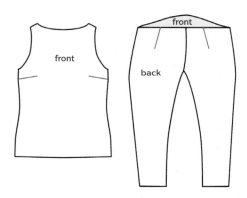

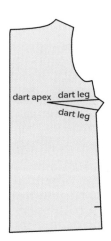

I provide step-by-step instructions for the bust dart method on page 87. The easiest way to figure out where to place lower body darts is to add extra inches to the waist, pinch the extra fabric on each side of your lower body above the fullest part of your buttocks, and mark it on the muslin. You can then transfer the markings to your sloper.

Sewing darts is easy! I like to mark the dart legs on the wrong side of the fabric first. Then you simply align the dart legs by pinching the fabric together with right sides facing, press, and place a pin at or otherwise mark the apex (this is optional; I can never see where the apex is while I'm sewing without the pin). Starting at the base of the dart (the widest part, not the apex), backstitch a few times and then sew along the dart leg marking. When you get close to the apex, remove the pin, and just keep sewing right off of the edge without backstitching, leaving a thread tail of about 5 to 6 inches. Tie a knot at the dart apex to secure and trim the thread. There's no need to trim the folded, extra fabric; just press that dart downward.

For muslin purposes, you don't need to tie a knot at the apex and can simply backstitch and move on.

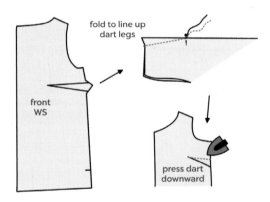

EASE

Ease is the extra measurement we'll be adding to the pattern pieces. If you tried to wear a garment made strictly from the base measurements of your body, you would feel like you'd been bundled into a straitjacket, completely immobilized (unless it's made out of knit fabric, and we'll address that for specific knit projects). I've included recommended wearing ease, but really play around with these numbers to figure out what feels comfortable for you. Ease is very much a personal preference. But you may be thinking, "What does that even mean? I want to know exactly how things should fit!" In broad terms, you want the sloper muslins to follow the silhouette of your body without being skintight, enabling you to move your limbs freely.

There's also style ease, which refers to the style or design that's part of drafting the garments themselves. One example of style ease is the Knit Cocoon Tunic Dress on page 175, which is designed to have generous proportions.

Ease can get confusing in the world of sewing. In more advanced pattern-making, you may have two pattern pieces that are intentionally mismatched (the inseam of a pants pattern, for example), but one piece is meant to be gently stretched to correspond to the other piece. That's called "easing in." This generally won't be part of the instructions for this book, though sometimes it's unavoidable with sleeves and inseams, and I've included information on how to deal with it if it comes up. To learn more, check out the excellent drafting books in the Resources section on page 262.

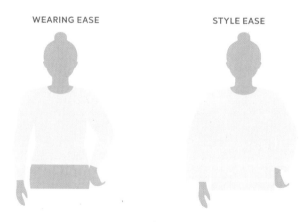

WEARING EASE   STYLE EASE

SQUARING CORNERS

There are several sections of a pattern piece that will require right angles. Using the corner of a gridded ruler is a good way to check for right angles; if you happen to have a triangle or L-square ruler, feel free to use it. Note that you only need the right angle to extend about ¼–½ inch at each corner, after which the seam can curve to suit the design. If the corner isn't at 90 degrees, you end up with a weird pointy bit when the pattern piece is cut out or sewn together.

The main areas to make sure you have right angles are:

- Necklines at the center fold and at the inner and out shoulder corners
- Other corners either cut on the fold (see page 50) or where two pattern pieces are sewn together, especially hems and sleeve edges

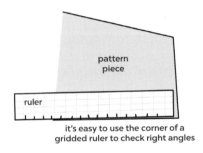

it's easy to use the corner of a
gridded ruler to check right angles

For example, if your neckline is not drawn at a right angle from the center line, it will end up looking like this:

Or this:

But you want it to look like this:

As you draft your slopers or patterns and sew them together, you'll start to notice when areas need to be squared. You will see a pink square any time a corner needs to be squared, like so:

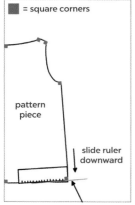

square the corner by sliding ruler along side until the ruler intersects about ⅓ to ½ of the hem and draw a line

You'll also notice that the hem will need to be curved slightly after the corner has been squared because a sharp angle forms at the line that intersects the hem from the right angle.

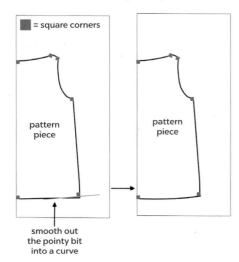

smooth out the pointy bit into a curve

Alright, now let's move on to measurements!

MEASUREMENTS

You will need:

- Enough elastic to tie around your waist
- Gridded ruler
- Necklace chain or similar
- Tape
- Measuring tape
- Mirror

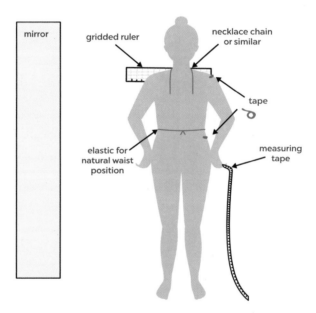

You'll also need your favorite note-taking supplies for writing down your measurements, or you can go to my website at SanaeIshida.com to download and print a handy-dandy chart with space for writing every measurement you'll need. I've broken down the measurements required per sloper, but you may want to tackle getting all the numbers in one fell swoop, which is great too!

So let's talk about the—gulp—measuring tape. When I was learning to do this, the number of measurements required seemed nearly infinite and the instructions always emphasized how I needed to have someone else measure me for super accurate numbers. I'm here to tell you that A) you can measure yourself, no problem; B) I've tried to streamline the work as much as possible, though there are still quite a few measurements to take; and C) accuracy is fantastic, but let's face it, our bodies change from day to day (at least mine seems to) and the projects in this book are not meant to yield clothes with corset-like fit. We're aiming for a fit that feels lovely and comfortable without sacrificing style.

All slopers begin with taking some measurements. Following is a list of everything that'll get you started and a few illustrations to guide you through the process of measuring yourself. Don't rush, but don't get too focused on exactitude either. Of course, if you've got a (patient and non-judgmental) person willing to help out, the whole thing will go a lot faster, but it's absolutely not necessary. I'm going to warn you that some of the body contortions involved in self-measurement will feel awkward, but I was soon laughing at myself, so my best tip is this: don't take yourself too seriously. It'll all be over before you know it.

WHAT TO WEAR

You want to wear your usual undergarments, and something snug but not too tight over that. Something like a knit tank top or cami/undershirt with leggings works well, and if they have side seams, all the better. I have seen many a sewing-book model in a leotard, but I don't own a leotard *or* a body suit, and maybe you don't either. If you want to do away with any kind of clothing to measure yourself, go for it. A vital note: make sure to wear the kind of undergarments you plan on wearing with your newly stitched-up wardrobe. My rule of thumb is to wear the best-fitting and most comfortable undergarments I own. Underwear doesn't usually have a huge effect—unless you prefer Spanx—but the fit of a bra will make a dramatic difference in the fit of the garment, so take heed.

Now let's begin measuring and drafting some slopers!

THE TORSO SLOPER

TORSO SLOPER MEASUREMENTS

As you can see from my torso slopers, the pattern pieces are drafted on the fold (see page 50), which means only half of the front and half of the back is required to create your muslin.

Note: some of the measurements that you take for the torso sloper will also be used in the sleeve and lower body torsos, and many of the measurements will be used repeatedly within each sloper section (e.g. the vertical measurements will be mostly the same for the front and back slopers), so I recommend drafting the slopers in the order I've provided here.

To create the torso sloper pattern pieces, we are going to measure the torso vertically and horizontally, and then we'll plot the points on paper and add armhole curves.

PREPPING FOR MEASUREMENTS

1. Start by draping the necklace (or your alternate item) around your neck. The ends can hang loose at the front of your body. The necklace will naturally rest where your neck meets your shoulder, which we'll call the *neck/shoulder point*.

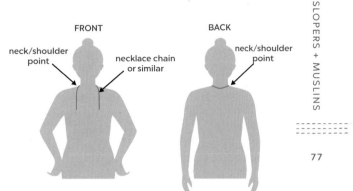

FRONT
BACK

neck/shoulder point
necklace chain or similar
neck/shoulder point

2. Tie the elastic around your waist. The elastic should be figure-hugging but not so tight that it's cutting off circulation. Bend your torso side-to-side, as if you're singing "I'm a little teapot" (or doing a side bend). Your sides will naturally crease and fold, and the elastic should settle into the creased section. We'll call this your *natural waist*.

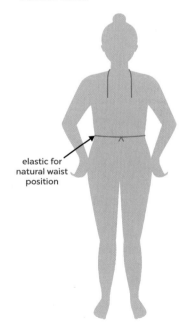

elastic for natural waist position

3 We'll be adding pieces of tape along the side of your body for reference points to measure. First, look in the mirror and see if one shoulder is higher than the other. If so, place the tape pieces on that side since it's easier to remove fabric for the lower shoulder if necessary. (It's probably not necessary. My right shoulder is markedly higher than my left, and I haven't needed to adjust patterns to accommodate it.) Please keep in mind that all bodies are wonderfully different and the illustrations included are for guidance purposes, but the actual tape placements, etc. will vary.

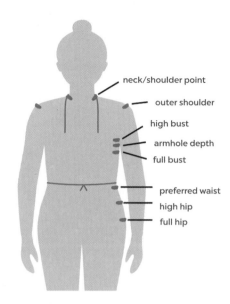

neck/shoulder point
outer shoulder
high bust
armhole depth
full bust
preferred waist
high hip
full hip

Place pieces of tape on the following:

- Hollow of neck—you may not need to mark the hollow of your neck, as it's generally easy to find when you need it: it's the spot in the center that dips inward between your clavicles.
- Neck/shoulder point—the necklace or chain may shift as you do, so I found it useful to place a piece of tape to mark the neck/shoulder points on both sides. Note that the neck/shoulder tape pieces will not be shown in subsequent illustrations.
- Outer shoulder—lift your arm up and down at the side to determine where your shoulder joint is. You should feel it moving up and down, and when your arm is up, there is typically an indentation on your shoulder. The tape should go right where the indentation is, centered on top of your shoulder. Do the same for the other shoulder.
- High bust/back—equivalent to the highest point of your armpit. We will use the same vertical measurement for the back. Place a piece a tape at the top of your armpit.

- Armhole depth—mark where you would like the bottom of the armhole to sit, often between your high bust and full bust. A helpful reference is the bottom of a T-shirt armhole. You'll use this measurement for the sleeve sloper too, FYI.
- Full bust/mid back—place the tape at the side where it corresponds to the fullest part of your chest. We will use the same vertical measurement for the mid back.
- Bust apex—the area that usually corresponds to where your nipple is, at the most prominent or fullest part of the bust. You may not need (or want) to put tape here, but feel free to do so for a '90s-era Madonna moment.
- Preferred waist—where you like to wear the waistband of your pants, shorts, or skirts. For some people this is the same as your natural waist, which is indicated by the elastic in step 2.
- High hip—where your pelvic bone is.
- Full hip—sometimes called low hip, this is the fullest part of your hip, including the buttocks.

VERTICAL MEASUREMENTS

Using the tape pieces, necklace, and elastic as visual reference points, measure vertically from the neck/shoulder point (unless otherwise noted) and record each of the following measurements. Keep the measuring tape as straight as possible vertically, though if you get a little bit of the curvature of your bust or belly, that's fine. Most of these measurements will also be used for the back torso sloper. There are diagrams of all the vertical measurements to take. Specific instructions for each individual measurement follow.

- Neck/shoulder point—you do not need to record the vertical measurement, since it is the starting point
- Hollow of neck
- High bust—where the armpit tape is (will also be used for back)
- Armhole depth—measure from outer shoulder tape to armhole depth tape
- Full bust (will also be used for mid back)
- Bust apex
- Natural waist
- Preferred waist
- High hip
- Full hip
- Shoulder slope depth

ARMHOLE DEPTH

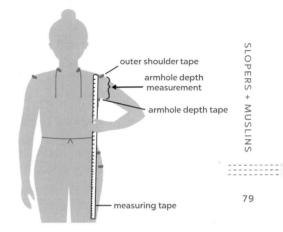

outer shoulder tape

armhole depth measurement

armhole depth tape

measuring tape

HOLLOW OF NECK

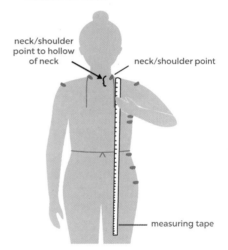

neck/shoulder point to hollow of neck

neck/shoulder point

measuring tape

FRONT

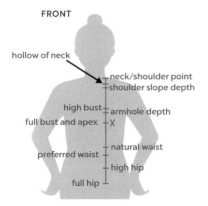

hollow of neck

neck/shoulder point
shoulder slope depth

high bust
full bust and apex
armhole depth
X

preferred waist
natural waist

high hip

full hip

BACK

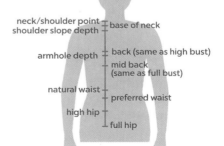

neck/shoulder point
shoulder slope depth
base of neck

armhole depth
back (same as high bust)
mid back (same as full bust)

natural waist

preferred waist

high hip

full hip

To get the shoulder slope depth, which you will need to draft your shoulder slope, place the gridded ruler against the front of your body so that it's horizontally level and positioned with the top edge at your neck/shoulder point.

Record the vertical distance between neck/shoulder point and the outer shoulder, which we are calling the *shoulder slope depth*. We will record the shoulder slope length in the next section to make sure that the back and front shoulder lengths will be the same.

HORIZONTAL MEASUREMENTS

Initially, we need the full circumference for most of the torso sections, and then we'll measure just the front— this is where the side seam on your tank top comes in handy—so you can calculate the back measurements. The only area that you'll measure separately is the shoulder. I've found that the shoulder dimensions get unwieldy when the circumference method is used.

To the right are diagrams of all the horizontal measurements to take. Specific instructions for each individual measurement follow.

SHOULDER SLOPE DEPTH

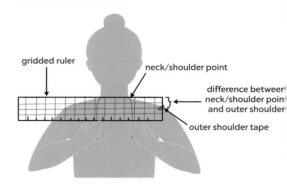

gridded ruler

neck/shoulder point

difference between neck/shoulder point and outer shoulder

outer shoulder tape

FRONT

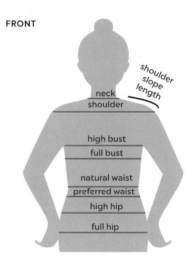

shoulder slope length

neck
shoulder

high bust
full bust

natural waist
preferred waist
high hip

full hip

BACK

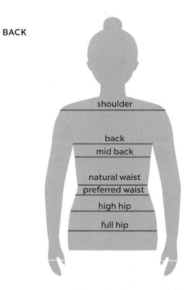

shoulder

back
mid back

natural waist
preferred waist

high hip

full hip

HORIZONTAL FULL MEASUREMENTS

Wrap the measuring tape horizontally around your torso. Arrange it to be snug but not so tight that you're cutting off circulation. You also want to make sure that the measuring tape doesn't get twisted, so take a peek in the mirror to double-check. Don't worry about the armhole depth horizontal measurements for the time being. We will deal with it during the drafting phase.

Take the following measurements:
- High bust circumference
- Full bust circumference
- Natural waist circumference
- Preferred waist circumference
- High hip circumference
- Full hip circumference

HORIZONTAL FRONT MEASUREMENTS

Now we'll get the front measurements. Using the necklace, tape pieces, and side seams (if available) as a guide, measure from side to side unless otherwise indicated. If you aren't wearing a garment with side seams, approximate where side seams would be and add tape there if you'd like.
- Neck—the width across the front of your neck; measure from one side of the necklace to the other
- Shoulder—outer shoulder to outer shoulder
- Shoulder slope length—neck/shoulder point to outer shoulder, as shown
- High bust
- Full bust
- Bust apex to bust apex (i.e. nipple to nipple), as shown
- Natural waist
- Preferred waist
- High hip
- Full hip

SHOULDER SLOPE LENGTH

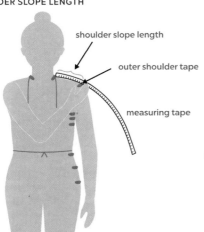

shoulder slope length

outer shoulder tape

measuring tape

BUST APEX TO BUST APEX

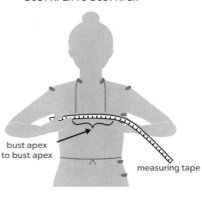

bust apex to bust apex

measuring tape

HORIZONTAL BACK MEASUREMENTS

Now we'll take one back measurement and calculate the rest.

- Shoulder—outer shoulder to outer shoulder. Secure the measuring tape to one outer shoulder by holding or taping it in place, then drape the measuring tape across the back to the other outer shoulder.

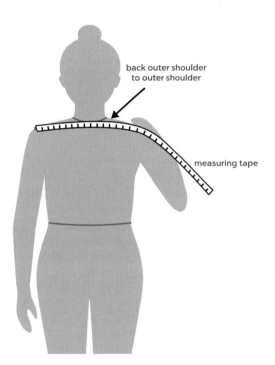

back outer shoulder
to outer shoulder

measuring tape

Calculate the following by subtracting horizontal front measurements from the corresponding circumferences:

- Back—corresponds to high bust on front. Subtract high bust from high bust circumference.
- Mid back—corresponds to full bust on front. Subtract full bust from full bust circumference.
- Natural waist
- Preferred waist
- High hip
- Full hip

Whew, you did it! You have all the measurements you need to get started on your torso sloper! If you want to go ahead and get your measurements for your sleeve sloper at this point, see page 97 (this way, you won't have to re-tape your upper body).

DRAFT THE TORSO SLOPER

We are going to draft just half of the front sloper and half of the back sloper; these will be traced onto fabric on the fold to create your muslins. The steps are virtually the same for the front and back slopers and if you want, you could draft them side by side along the same horizontal lines. If you don't have wide enough paper, or if it's easier to draft them individually, that's great too!

FRONT TORSO SLOPER

You'll plot the following points based on your measurements.

1 Draft the center fold line. Draw a vertical line equal to the neck/shoulder point to full hip vertical measurement. You may want to place this line toward the left side of the paper, since you'll add horizontal lines extending toward the right side:

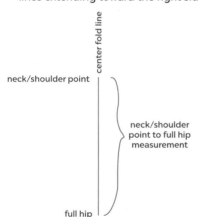

2 Mark the following *vertical* measurements on the line:
- Neck/shoulder point—the topmost point
- Hollow of neck
- Shoulder slope depth
- High bust
- Armhole depth—don't forget that you measured this from the outer shoulder, which is where the shoulder depth slope is marked. So if the armhole depth was 5 inches from the outer shoulder, mark 5 inches below the shoulder slope depth position.
- Full bust
- Natural waist
- Preferred waist
- High hip
- Full hip

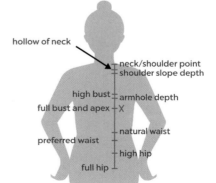

3 We're going to do a little bit of math now. Since we are drafting a sloper that is half of the front body, we'll divide the following horizontal front measurements in half.

Divide by 2:
- Neck—width between chain
- Shoulder—outer shoulder to outer shoulder
- High bust—side to side
- Armhole depth—use the same measurement as full bust below
- Full bust—side to side
- Bust apex to bust apex
- Natural waist—side to side
- Preferred waist—side to side
- High hip—side to side
- Full hip—side to side

Then add the recommended ease to the divided measurements from above (see page 71 for ease information). After you try your muslin, you will most likely want to adjust this ease depending on your body shape and fit of the sloper. Some people prefer more ease, others like less. For bust sizes DD and above, you may want to consider adding a dart (see page 87) and additional ease.

Add ease amount:
- High bust: ¼ inch
- Armhole depth: ½ inch
- Full bust: ½ inch
- Natural waist: ¼ inch
- Preferred waist: ¼ inch
- High hip: ¼ inch
- Full hip: ¼ inch

4 Using the final measurements from step 3 (including ease), draw horizontal lines from the center fold line as shown.

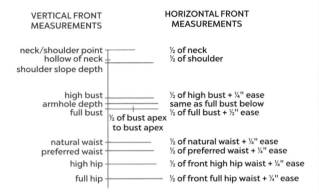

VERTICAL FRONT MEASUREMENTS

neck/shoulder point
hollow of neck
shoulder slope depth

high bust
armhole depth
full bust
½ of bust apex to bust apex

natural waist
preferred waist
high hip
full hip

HORIZONTAL FRONT MEASUREMENTS

½ of neck
½ of shoulder

½ of high bust + ¼" ease
same as full bust below
½ of full bust + ½" ease

½ of natural waist + ¼" ease
½ of preferred waist + ¼" ease
½ of front high hip waist + ¼" ease
½ of front full hip waist + ¼" ease

5 Draw the neckline curve. Make sure that the neckline is perpendicular (at a right angle) to the center fold line for at least ½ inch. This is called "squaring" (see page 72). Using a French curve or styling design curve will help create a smooth neckline, but you could also freehand this. Note: if the neck opening seems too small to fit your head, you can enlarge it by lowering the neckline point at the center fold line and adjusting the curve. Alternatively, you can leave a portion of the shoulder unsewn during the muslin stage.

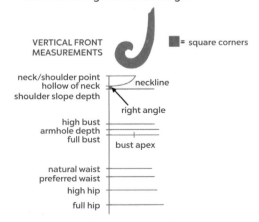

VERTICAL FRONT MEASUREMENTS

■ = square corners

neck/shoulder point
hollow of neck
shoulder slope depth

neckline
right angle

high bust
armhole depth
full bust
bust apex

natural waist
preferred waist
high hip
full hip

6 Draw the shoulder slope. Connect the neck/shoulder point to the shoulder slope depth endpoint. Square the corner where the shoulder line meets the neck/shoulder point. Check the length of the line you drew against your shoulder slope measurement. It should be the same, or at least close. Note: I like to draw this as a straight line, but some people find that a slight curve fits their shoulder better.

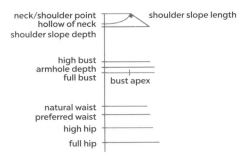

VERTICAL FRONT
MEASUREMENTS

The armhole is best adjusted in the muslin phase, so don't stress too much about the curve! Square the corner as shown.

8 Connect the endpoints of each line from the armhole depth down—armhole depth, full bust, natural waist, preferred waist, high hip, and full hip—to shape the side edge. You'll want to redraw sharp angles between the full bust and full hip into a smooth curve. Notice that a little more ease has been added to the high hip line when smoothing the curve, and that's okay. Square underarm as shown.

VERTICAL FRONT
MEASUREMENTS

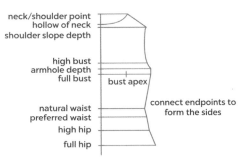

connect endpoints to form the sides

7 Shape the armhole curve by connecting the shoulder slope depth endpoint to the armhole depth line endpoint (a). Again, a French curve/styling design curve is super helpful here, though it's definitely manageable without one.

VERTICAL FRONT
MEASUREMENTS

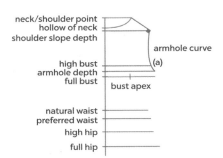

armhole curve

(a)

VERTICAL FRONT
MEASUREMENTS

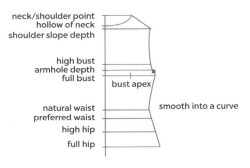

smooth into a curve

(9) If you want to add a dart, skip to Adding a Bust Dart on page 87. Otherwise, draw the hem. Measure the width of the drafted front sloper at the high bust and the second widest measurement above the full hip, which will most likely be your full bust. Subtract the high bust from the full bust (or second widest measurement). Measure that amount from the bottom of the center line and make a mark. Draw a curve from the marking to the end of the full hip line, making sure to square both ends of the line.

VERTICAL FRONT MEASUREMENTS

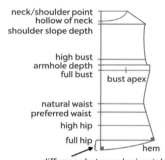

neck/shoulder point
hollow of neck
shoulder slope depth

high bust
armhole depth
full bust

bust apex

natural waist
preferred waist
high hip
full hip

hem

difference between horizontal front measurements of high bust and full bust (or second widest measurement)

(10) Double-check that corners are squared as shown, add grainline (see page 48), label your work "front torso sloper," and cut out.

VERTICAL FRONT MEASUREMENTS

neck/shoulder point
hollow of neck
shoulder slope depth

FRONT TORSO SLOPER

high bust
armhole depth
full bust

bust apex

fold

natural waist
preferred waist
high hip
full hip

grainline

FINISHED FRONT TORSO SLOPER

FRONT TORSO SLOPER

bust apex

fold

grainline

ADDING A BUST DART

If you want the extra shaping of a bust dart, here are instructions. You'll want to incorporate the dart once you've gotten to step 9. In case you want to dive deeply into adding darts and general bust adjustments, I have added materials in the Resources section on page 262.

1 Draw the following lines on your front pattern piece:
- A to B—vertical line parallel to grainline from bust apex to hem.
- A to C—horizontal line from bust apex to side, perpendicular to AB.
- A to D—diagonal line from bust apex to a point about a third of the way up the armhole.

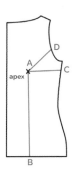

2 On a separate piece of paper, draw 2 parallel vertical lines slightly longer than the vertical line labeled AB above and separated by an additional ¼ for every cup size up, starting with ¼ inch between the lines for A and B cups.
- A and B = ¼ inch
- C = ½ inch
- D = ¾ inch
- DD = 1 inch

Beyond DD, it's advisable to add a little bit more to the bodice width first—start with about ½ inch.

3 Cut your sloper to widen. Starting at the hem, cut along lines B to A and A to D, but stop before the armhole. Leave a small amount uncut at D, which will become a hinge.

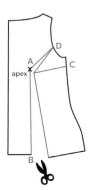

4 Cut, starting from the side this time, from C to A, but stop before the bust apex point. Leave a small amount uncut at A, which will be another hinge.

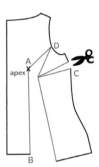

5 Position the paper with the parallel lines beneath the cut-apart sloper and line up as shown. Tape sloper in place. The dart should automatically form.

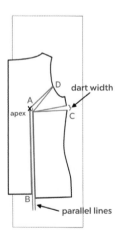

6 Because you don't want your dart to end right at the bust apex, we'll move it slightly. Measure the dart width at its base. Now, draw a new line perpendicular to line AB from A to E. Starting at point E, measure the distance of the dart width toward the hem, and mark point F.

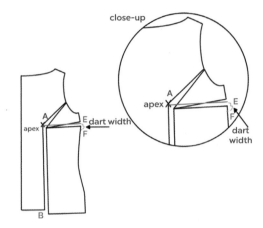

7 About 1 to 1½ inches from the bust apex on the armhole side, mark point G on line AE.

8 Draw a diagonal line from F to G. This is your new dart: the apex is at G, and the legs are lines GE and GF.

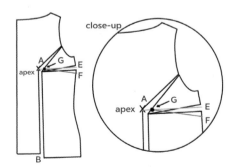

9 Redraw the hem line.

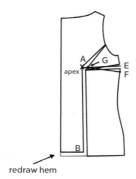

redraw hem

10 Curve hem and square corners (see page 72).

11 Add grainline (see page 48), label your work "front torso sloper," and cut out.

Your front sloper is now complete! (We are not adding seam allowances at this time.)

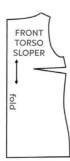

FRONT
TORSO
SLOPER

fold

BACK TORSO SLOPER

Drafting the back sloper is essentially the same as the front sloper (except for the dart section, if you did that), but we'll be using the back measurements this time.

1 Draft the center fold line. Draw a vertical line equal to the neck/shoulder point to full hip vertical measurement. You may want to place the line closer to the left edge of the paper since you'll add horizontal lines extending toward the right side:

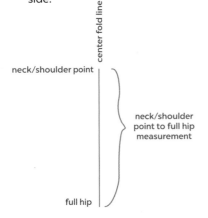

center fold line

neck/shoulder point

neck/shoulder point to full hip measurement

full hip

2 Mark the following vertical measurements on the line:
- Neck/shoulder point—the topmost point
- Base of neck—you did not get a measurement for this. Mark a spot 1½ inches down from the neck/shoulder point.
- Shoulder slope depth
- Back—use high bust from front sloper
- Armhole depth—use measurement calculated for front sloper
- Mid back—use full bust from front sloper
- Natural waist
- Preferred waist
- High hip
- Full hip

VERTICAL MEASUREMENTS
BACK

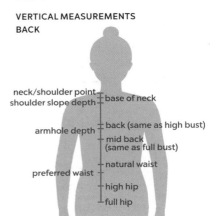

neck/shoulder point
shoulder slope depth
base of neck

armhole depth
back (same as high bust)
mid back (same as full bust)
natural waist

preferred waist
high hip
full hip

3 Math time again! Remember, we are drafting a sloper that represents half of the back of the body. To get most of the back measurements, you subtracted the front side-to-side measurements from the circumference. We are now dividing the resulting horizontal measurements in half.

Divide by 2:
- Neck—use the neck measurement from front sloper
- Back shoulder—outer shoulder to outer shoulder
- Back
- Armhole depth—use the same measurement as mid back (below)
- Mid back
- Natural waist
- Preferred waist
- High hip
- Full hip

Then add the recommended ease to the divided measurements from above. After you try your muslin, you will most likely want to adjust this ease depending on your body shape and fit of the sloper.

Sewing Love

Some people prefer more ease, others like less.

Add ease amount:
- Back: ¼ inch
- Armhole depth: ½ inch
- Mid back: ½ inch
- Natural waist: ¼ inch
- Preferred waist: ¼ inch
- High hip: ¼ inch
- Full hip: ¼ inch

4 Using the final measurements (including ease) from step 3, draw horizontal lines from the center fold line as shown.

VERTICAL BACK MEASUREMENTS	HORIZONTAL FRONT MEASUREMENTS
neck/shoulder point hollow of neck shoulder slope depth	½ of neck ½ of back shoulder
back (same as high bust) armhole depth mid back (same as full bust)	½ of back + ¼" ease same as mid back below ½ of full bust + ½" ease
natural waist preferred waist high hip full hip	½ of back nat. waist + ¼" ease ½ of back pref. waist + ¼" ease ½ of back high hip + ¼" ease ½ of back hip + ¼" ease

5 Draw the shoulder slope. Something to keep in mind is that the back outer shoulder width tends to be bigger than the corresponding front measurement, but the shoulder slope length will need to be the same for both the front and back slopers. A good way to make them match is to use the shoulder slope measurement from the front sloper.

First, measure the shoulder slope length on your front sloper (or use the measurement you took before). On the back sloper pattern, starting at the shoulder slope depth line endpoint (a), draw a diagonal line equal to that measurement toward the neck/shoulder point (b). Because the line is based on the shorter front shoulder measurement, it may not reach the neck/shoulder point line on the back, and that's fine.

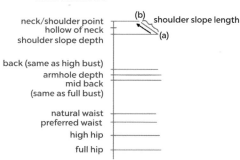

VERTICAL BACK
MEASUREMENTS

neck/shoulder point
hollow of neck
shoulder slope depth

back (same as high bust)
armhole depth
mid back
(same as full bust)

natural waist
preferred waist
high hip
full hip

(b) shoulder slope length
(a)

6 Draw the neckline curve. Connect the base of the neck marking to the shoulder line you drew in step 5. Make sure that the neckline is perpendicular (at a right angle) to the center fold line for at least ½ inch (see page 72). Using a French curve or styling design curve will help create a smooth neckline, but you could also freehand this. Square the corner of the shoulder as well.

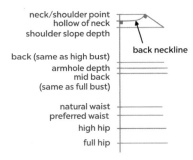

7 Shape the armhole curve. Again, a French curve is super helpful here, though you can absolutely freehand this. The back armhole curve tends to be a little flatter than the front:

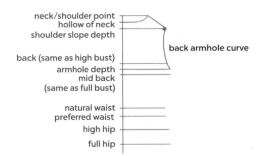

This, however, completely depends on your body shape and what feels comfortable. The armhole is best adjusted in the muslin phase, so don't stress too much about the curve!

Make sure to square the corner at the outer shoulder.

8 Connect the endpoints of each line from the armhole depth down—armhole depth, mid back, natural waist, preferred waist, high hip, and full hip—to shape the side edge. You'll want to redraw any sharp angles between armhole depth and full hip into a smooth curve. Square underarm as shown.

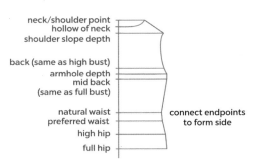

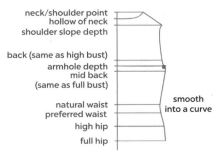

9 Draw the hem. Measure the width of the drafted back sloper at the high hip and full hip. Subtract the high hip from the full hip. Measure that amount from the bottom of the center line and make a mark.

Draw a curve from the marking to the end of the full hip line, making sure to square both ends of the line.

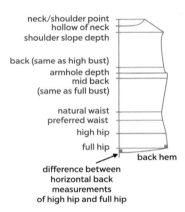

VERTICAL BACK
MEASUREMENTS

neck/shoulder point
hollow of neck
shoulder slope depth

back (same as high bust)
armhole depth
mid back
(same as full bust)

natural waist
preferred waist
high hip
full hip

back hem

difference between
horizontal back
measurements
of high hip and full hip

10 Align (see page 67) the back sloper against the front sloper. Make sure that the shoulders, armholes at the top and bottom (the armhole curves will usually be different lengths), sides, and hems match up.

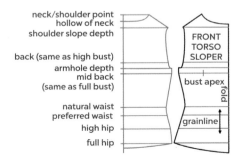

VERTICAL BACK
MEASUREMENTS

neck/shoulder point
hollow of neck
shoulder slope depth

back (same as high bust)
armhole depth
mid back
(same as full bust)

natural waist
preferred waist
high hip
full hip

FRONT
TORSO
SLOPER

bust apex

grainline

11 Add grainline, double-check squared corners, label your work "back torso sloper," and cut out.

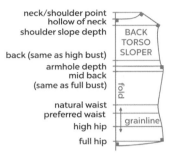

VERTICAL BACK
MEASUREMENTS

neck/shoulder point
hollow of neck
shoulder slope depth

back (same as high bust)
armhole depth
mid back
(same as full bust)

natural waist
preferred waist
high hip
full hip

BACK
TORSO
SLOPER

fold

grainline

Your back sloper is now complete! (We are not adding seam allowances at this time.)

FINISHED BACK
TORSO SLOPER

BACK
TORSO
SLOPER

fold

grainline

TORSO MUSLIN

1 Press your muslin or cotton fabric.

2 Place paper sloper patterns on the fabric and trace. You will trace one front piece and one back piece on the fold (see page 50). Make sure to mark which is which on the fabric. If you added darts, transfer the dart markings (note that darts are not included in illustrations). Add ⅝-inch seam allowance (see page 67) to the shoulders and side seams. Don't worry about the neckline, armhole, or hem for now. Cut out.

3 If applicable, sew darts (see page 69). Then with right sides facing, machine-baste the shoulder seams with a ⅝-inch seam allowance. Consider leaving half of one shoulder unsewn if the neck opening seems too small. Sew one side all the way from the bottom of the armhole to the hem. On the other side, either leave the entire side unsewn or only sew about a third of the way down from the bottom of the armhole.

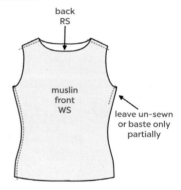

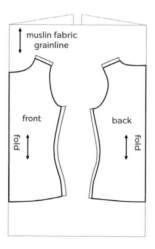

COMMON TORSO FIT ISSUES

Let's check the fit! Gaping, tightness, and shoulder seam issues are the most common. Assess the fit of your muslin, mark any adjustments directly on the muslin, and then transfer the markings to your sloper. See page 59 for how to transfer markings. For additional fitting resources, see page 262.

GAPING: If the gaping is significant and using the method below distorts the curve too much, consider adding a dart (see page 87).

TOO TIGHT: The most common area of tightness is the armhole, and the following method of cutting and spreading will add ease.

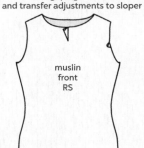

pinch excess gaping, mark on muslin, and transfer adjustments to sloper

muslin
front
RS

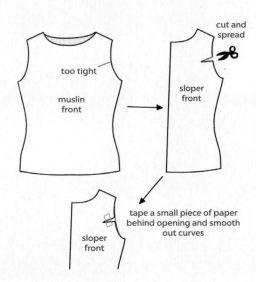

cut and spread

too tight

muslin
front

sloper
front

sloper
front

tape a small piece of paper behind opening and smooth out curves

SHOULDER SEAM IS TOO FAR BACK: Most people have shoulders that roll forward, and you may need to adjust for that. First measure how much the shoulder seam needs to be shifted on the muslin, then add that amount to the back sloper shoulder section and remove the same amount from the front sloper like so:

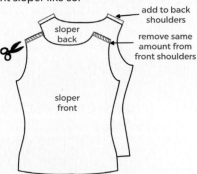

add to back shoulders

sloper
back

remove same amount from front shoulders

sloper
front

SLEEVE SLOPER MEASUREMENTS

The sleeve sloper measurements are relatively straightforward, though there's a tiny bit more math involved than the torso sloper. It's still easy math, though! Unlike the torso and lower body slopers, which are half-pieces, we will draft the full sleeve here.

PREPPING FOR MEASUREMENTS
Place tape pieces as specified below for vertical and horizontal measurements.

- Outer shoulder—you should have already marked this spot with tape for the front sloper, but if you haven't, lift your arm up and down at the side to determine where your shoulder joint is. You should feel it moving up and down, and when your arm is up, there is typically an indentation on your shoulder. Place a piece of tape to mark the joint. One side is fine for the sleeve sloper, whereas you mark both shoulders for the torso sloper.
- Armhole depth—you should already have this measurement from the torso sloper (measured from the outer shoulder, which is what you'll be doing here as well), but if you don't, mark where you would like the bottom of the armhole to be, usually between your high bust/top of armpit and full bust. A helpful reference is the bottom of a T-shirt armhole.
- Elbow—place tape on the bone at the bottom of your elbow.
- Wrist—place tape on your wrist bone.

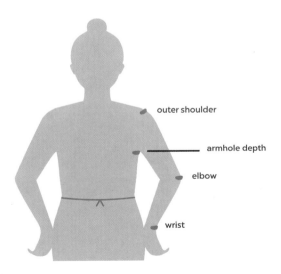

outer shoulder

armhole depth

elbow

wrist

Sewing Love

VERTICAL MEASUREMENTS

Here are the vertical measurements that you will need:

- Outer arm length—outer shoulder to wrist bone, with your arm slightly bent. Securing the measuring tape at the wrist and gently guiding the measuring tape up to the outer shoulder edge works best for me.
- Armhole depth—you will have this number if you already created your torso sloper. See page 78 for measuring directions.
- Shoulder to elbow—outer shoulder edge to elbow, with your arm slightly bent.

VERTICAL SLEEVE MEASUREMENT

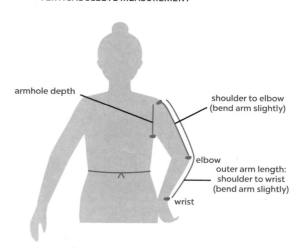

armhole depth

shoulder to elbow
(bend arm slightly)

elbow

outer arm length:
shoulder to wrist
(bend arm slightly)

wrist

HORIZONTAL MEASUREMENTS

Wrap the measuring tape snugly around your arm to get the following horizontal measurements:

- Bicep circumference—or fullest part of arm. Take a measurement with your arm relaxed, then make a muscle to see if the circumference changes. Record the larger number.
- Elbow circumference
- Wrist circumference

Fairly painless, right? Let's move on to drafting the sleeve sloper!

HORIZONTAL SLEEVE MEASUREMENT

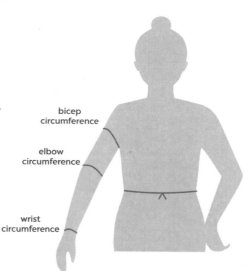

bicep
circumference

elbow
circumference

wrist
circumference

DRAFT THE SLEEVE SLOPER

I tried many methods to draft a sleeve sloper, and found the ikatbag.com method the most helpful, but I've made my own modifications to simplify the steps. Once the sleeve sloper is drafted, you'll need to make sure that it fits the armhole of the torso sloper, so there will be some additional tweaking to be made in the muslin stage.

1. Draw a vertical line equal to the length of the outer arm measurement and mark the following vertical measurements on the line. Add the label "front" to the left side, and "back" to the right side.

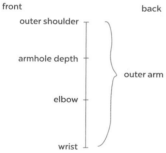

VERTICAL
MEASUREMENTS

- Outer shoulder—the topmost point
- Armhole depth
- Elbow
- Wrist

2. Add the ease amounts below to the horizontal measurements for bicep, elbow, and wrist. Center the horizontal lines on the vertical points. Notice that you will use the bicep plus ease measurement at the armhole depth point. We will call this the bicep line, though it is technically the bottom of the sleeve cap.

Add ease amount:
- Bicep: 1½ inches
- Elbow: 1½ inches
- Wrist: 1¾ inches

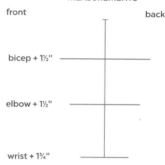

HORIZONTAL
MEASUREMENTS

3. Draw the sleeve. Connect the bicep and wrist endpoints; if the elbow line is shorter than the bicep line, ignore the elbow line and just make a straight line from bicep to wrist. Note: it's helpful to know where your elbow is located on the sloper when drafting garments, so we want to include it with the other information on the sloper:

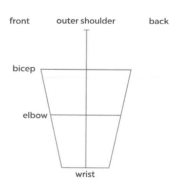

4 Let's do a little bit of math here to create a sleeve cap that accommodates our asymmetrical bodies. Divide the bicep line on the front half of the sleeve into 4 equal parts and mark the first (leftmost) segment "A":

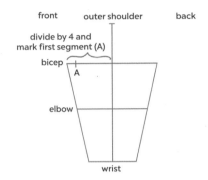

5 Divide the bicep line on the back half of the sleeve into 6 equal parts and mark the last (rightmost) segment "B":

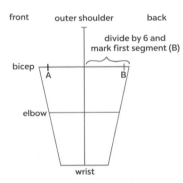

6 Measure the length of both segments and add them together. Draw a line extending from the outer shoulder point to the right (toward the back side of the sleeve) for "C" (A + B = C). Note: we'll use length A again in step 8, so you may want to write it down:

STEP 6

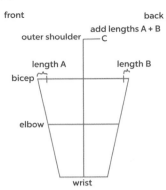

7 Multiply length C by 2 and draw a line extending to the left (front side) for "D":

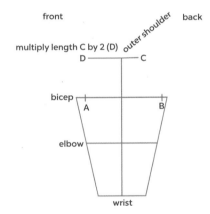

8 Connect point A to point D and mark a length up that line equal to the first segment of the front bicep line (length A). This will be point "E":

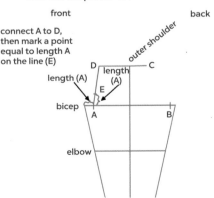

9 Connect point B to point C, then divide that line into 3 equal parts. Mark these "F" (upper point) and "G" (lower point):

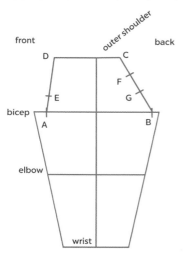

10 Using a French curve or freehand, draw curves for the sleeve cap as shown. Your curve may look different depending on your measurements:

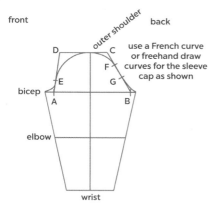

Square the corners at each side of the wrist (see page 72).

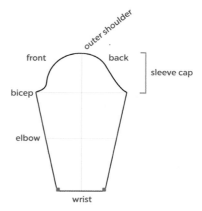

This method yields a pretty good starting point, though you'll still need to align it (see page 67) with the designated armhole and adjust the curve length to fit.

Note: The curve of the sleeve cap should be at least as long as the armhole measurement or up to an inch longer. If the sleeve cap curve is longer than the armhole curve, the sleeve can be eased into the armhole by either stretching the armhole or by adding two rows of basting stitches to the sleeve cap that will subtly gather the sleeve cap.

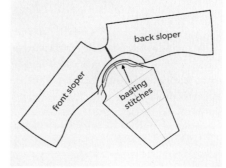

11 Add grainline and markings for front, center, and back. Label as "sleeve sloper" and cut out.

FINISHED SLEEVE SLOPER

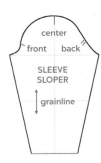

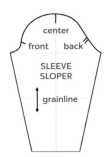

ABOUT SLEEVE CAP HEIGHT

The quick take: the taller the cap, the more fitted the sleeve. A more fitted sleeve means fewer wrinkles and puckers and more restricted arm and shoulder movements. Manufacturers prefer low, wider caps because they're easier to sew and fit. After trying many, many sleeves, I've found that a sleeve cap height of 5 to 6 inches works best for me, but as always, this is a personal preference. This illustration gives you a sense of range that different sleeve cap heights give:

When I raise or lower the sleeve cap, I simply redraw the curve (a French curve is great, but I usually freehand it), but there are a number of ways to do this, including the method I show for the Cardigan on page 233.

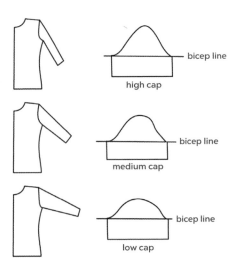

SLEEVE MUSLIN

1 Press your muslin or cotton fabric.

2 Place sleeve sloper on the fabric and trace. Add ⅝-inch seam allowance (see page 67) as shown.

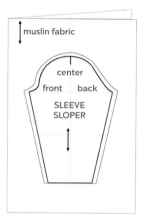

muslin fabric

center
front   back
SLEEVE
SLOPER

STEP 3

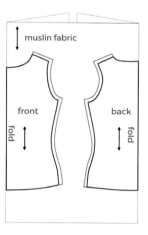

muslin fabric

front   back

fold   fold

3 You will need to create a new torso muslin, since you will be adding seam allowances for the sleeves. You could skip the torso muslin on pages 94–95 and fiddle with the torso and sleeve muslins in one go, but I find it easier to address all the torso sloper adjustments without sleeves, and the end result is a better overall fit.

Place torso sloper on the fabric and trace. If you added a dart to the front sloper, transfer dart markings as well (the illustrations in this section will not have a dart). Add ⅝-inch seam allowance to shoulders, sides and armholes.

4 If applicable, sew darts (see page 69). Then with right sides facing, machine baste the shoulder seams with a ⅝-inch seam allowance. Consider leaving half of one shoulder unsewn if the neck opening seems too small.

back
RS

if neck opening is
too small, sew only
half of shoulder

muslin
front
WS

5 With right sides together, machine baste the sleeve cap to the armhole with a ⅝-inch seam allowance. I like to sew both sleeves in because I've found the fit is different compared to having just one sewn in. Taking the muslin on and off will be a bit trickier when both sleeves are sewn in, however.

6 With right sides facing, machine baste along the bottom of the sleeve, pivot, and continue down the side with a ⅝-inch seam allowance. On the other side, either leave the entire side unsewn or only sew about ⅓ of the way down from the bottom of the armhole.

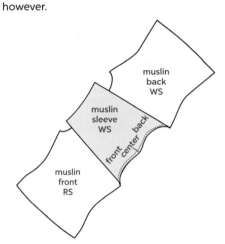

muslin back WS

muslin sleeve WS

front center back

muslin front RS

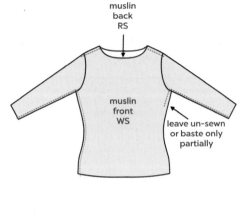

muslin back RS

muslin front WS

leave un-sewn or baste only partially

COMMON SLEEVE FIT ISSUES

How's the fit? Keep in mind that it's impossible to get rid of sleeve wrinkles and puckers entirely, but you will definitely notice when it's too tight or too loose.

SLEEVE CAP TOO TIGHT OR TOO LOOSE (BAGGY): You will see an excess of fabric around the armhole when the sleeve is too baggy. When it's too tight, diagonal lines will radiate from where the sleeve connects to the armhole.

Mark any adjustments directly on the muslin, and then transfer the markings to your sloper. See page 59 for how to transfer markings. For additional fitting resources, see page 262.

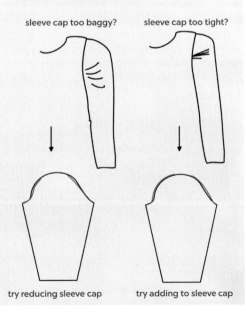

sleeve cap too baggy? sleeve cap too tight?

try reducing sleeve cap try adding to sleeve cap

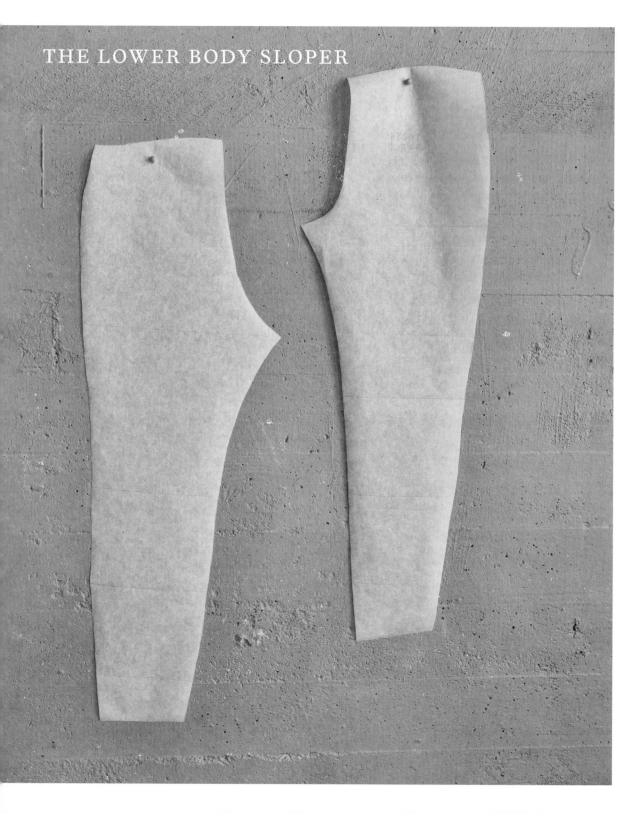

LOWER BODY SLOPER MEASUREMENTS

First, I want to point out again that the illustrations in this section and your actual lower body sloper may look different, since each and every body is unique. Now, drafting the lower body sloper requires a little spatial imagination because you will use one quarter of the circumference measurements from waist to hip, but from upper thigh to ankle, you'll use half of the circumference measurements. Here's a visual of how the lower body slopers relate to the body:

As you can see, the front sloper is only one half (or one quarter of the full pattern, as it's the front half for one leg), so you will be cutting out two pieces for the muslin. Same with the back sloper. Confused? I was too. As you follow the steps, it'll start to make sense.

That said, the trickiest bit with lower body sloper is actually the crotch curve. (The word "crotch" is not my favorite, and I've seen and heard the word "rise" used in its stead. While I rather like the sound of that, I will use crotch to avoid confusion because it's found in patterns more frequently.)

We'll be taking crotch measurements for both length and depth. Here's how the measurements will translate into sloper form:

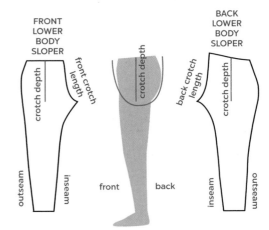

The crotch curve seam will be at the center of your body and will extend out in that funny way you've undoubtedly seen when folding laundry, which is what shapes four flat pieces of fabric into a three-dimensional garment to fit the stomach and hips.

Time to take some measurements!

PREPPING FOR MEASUREMENTS

If you've already measured yourself for the torso sloper, you'll have these measurements:

- Preferred waist
- High hip
- Full hip

If you haven't already taken these measurements, place tape pieces along the side of your body at all of the points below. If you already have the first three, start at upper thigh:

- Preferred waist—where you like to wear your pants, shorts, or skirts. For some people this is the same as the natural waist (for tips on finding your natural waist, see page 77).
- High hip—where your pelvic bone is.
- Full hip—sometimes called low hip, this is the fullest part of your hip, including the buttocks.
- Upper thigh—the fullest part of your upper leg, usually between ½ and 4 inches below your crotch/buttocks.
- Thigh—about halfway between the upper thigh and knee.
- Knee—at the top of your knee cap or where the bone juts out most.
- Calf—the fullest part of your calf.
- Ankle—at ankle bone.

Also, grab a chair with a hard seat (e.g. a wooden chair) so you can measure the crotch depth sitting down (no tape required).

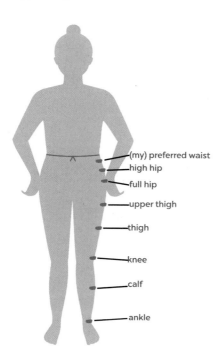

(my) preferred waist
high hip
full hip
upper thigh
thigh
knee
calf
ankle

VERTICAL LOWER BODY MEASUREMENTS

Measure from your preferred waist along the side of your body (unless otherwise noted), keeping the measuring tape as straight as possible. Record the measurements in your preferred format:

- High hip
- Full hip
- Upper thigh
- Thigh
- Knee
- Calf
- Outseam (from preferred waist to ankle bone)
- Inseam (from crotch to ankle bone)

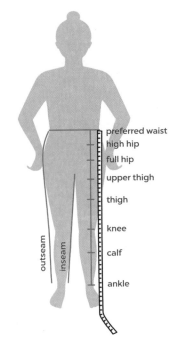

HORIZONTAL MEASUREMENTS

First, we'll wrap the measuring tape completely around each part for circumference measurements, then we'll measure just the front side of the lower body from side to side (a pair of leggings with side seams is very helpful for this). We'll calculate most of the back measurements by subtracting the front measurements from the circumference. Note that it's usually not necessary to measure both legs; we'll be adding enough ease that any small differences there may be between your legs won't be noticeable, but feel free to measure both legs if you'd like. Here is the full list of measurements, and instructions for each follow.

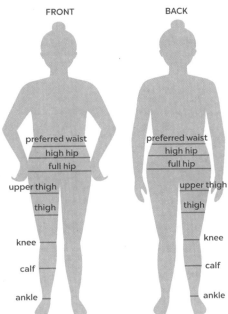

HORIZONTAL FULL MEASUREMENTS

If you already have the first three measurements from the torso sloper, start at the upper thigh:

- Preferred waist circumference
- High hip circumference
- Full hip circumference
- Upper thigh circumference
- Thigh circumference
- Knee circumference
- Calf circumference
- Ankle circumference

HORIZONTAL FRONT MEASUREMENTS

Use measurement from torso sloper if available. If not, measure from side to side on the front side only:

- Preferred waist
- High hip
- Full hip

HORIZONTAL BACK MEASUREMENTS

Use measurements from torso sloper if available. If not, calculate the following by subtracting each front horizontal measurement from the corresponding circumference:

- Preferred waist
- High hip
- Full hip

CROTCH MEASUREMENTS

CROTCH LENGTH

The crotch length is taken while standing with your legs slightly apart. Thread the measuring tape between your legs and draw it snugly up to your body. Measure from the preferred waist at the front, ending at the preferred waist in the back. It's helpful to record separate measurements for the front and back crotch lengths as well. You could tie a ribbon at, say, the 20-inch mark on the measuring tape and then hold the tape with the ribbon at the center of your crotch, and gauge the front and back measurements. If your leggings have an intersecting seam at the crotch, you could also use that as a reference point for the center.

CROTCH DEPTH

You'll want to sit down when measuring your crotch depth because the body spreads and shifts when sitting, and you want to account for that. If you were to sew pants based on your standing crotch depth, chances are good that your pants would cut off your circulation if you attempted to rest on a chair. It's easier to use the gridded ruler for this one, though a regular ruler is fine too. Sit down and set the short end of your ruler on the chair seat next to you on the same side as the tape marking your preferred waist reference point. The crotch depth is the distance between your preferred waist and the surface of the chair.

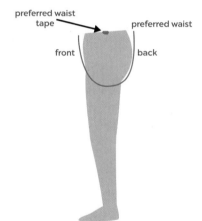

preferred waist tape
preferred waist
front   back

preferred waist tape

You're all set to start drafting your lower body sloper!

DRAFT THE LOWER BODY SLOPER

We are going to draft a front and a back sloper. Remember, each piece will be cut on folded fabric to create two mirrored pieces for a full front and a full back, so each sloper piece is going to be a quarter of the total pants.

For the initial draft of the sloper, you won't be adding darts, but will consider them in the muslin stage. In case you need to add darts in the muslin stage, the instructions allocate a couple of extra inches of ease to the waist here. If you have no derriere to speak of (like me),

consider skipping the extra ease for the darts. For most other sections, I recommend an ease of about ¼ inch. It's better to start off with less ease and add more, since it's harder to adjust a too-loose fit. See page 69 for dart information.

Like the torso sloper, feel free to draft the front and back lower body sloper pieces side by side if you have paper that is wide enough, or you can draft them one at a time. The instructions will address the front and back individually.

FRONT LOWER BODY SLOPER

1 Draw a vertical line equal to the outseam measurement. This will be the center line.

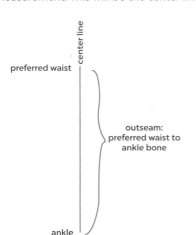

2 Plot the vertical points:
- Preferred waist—the topmost point
- High hip
- Full hip
- Crotch depth
- Upper thigh
- Thigh
- Knee
- Calf
- Ankle

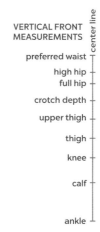

3 Divide the following measurements by 2. Remember that the front preferred waist, high hip, and full hip are the horizontal measurements taken for the front only, not the full circumference.

Divide by 2:
- Front preferred waist
- Front high hip
- Front full hip
- Upper thigh circumference
- Thigh circumference
- Knee circumference
- Calf circumference
- Ankle circumference

Now add the ease to each:
- Front preferred waist: ½ inch
- Front high hip: ¼ inch
- Front full hip: ¼ inch
- Upper thigh: ¼ inch
- Thigh: ¼ inch
- Knee: ½ inch
- Calf: ¼ inch
- Ankle: 1½ inches

4 Using the measurements you calculated for step 3 (including the ease), draw horizontal lines centered on the vertical points. We will address the crotch depth in the next step.

Sewing Love

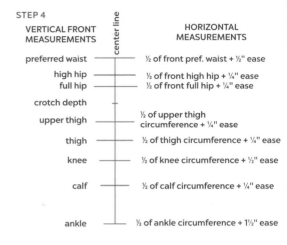

STEP 4

VERTICAL FRONT MEASUREMENTS — center line — HORIZONTAL MEASUREMENTS

preferred waist —— ½ of front pref. waist + ½" ease
high hip —— ½ of front high hip + ¼" ease
full hip —— ½ of front full hip + ¼" ease
crotch depth ——
upper thigh —— ½ of upper thigh circumference + ¼" ease
thigh —— ½ of thigh circumference + ¼" ease
knee —— ½ of knee circumference + ½" ease
calf —— ½ of calf circumference + ¼" ease
ankle —— ½ of ankle circumference + 1½" ease

5 For the crotch depth line, draw a horizontal line equal in length to the full hip line, then extend the line to the left about 2 inches. Depending on your crotch length, you may not need to use the entire extension in the next step, or you may need to add more. This extension is to give you a starting point.

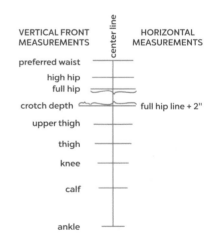

VERTICAL FRONT MEASUREMENTS — center line — HORIZONTAL MEASUREMENTS

preferred waist
high hip
full hip
crotch depth —— full hip line + 2"
upper thigh
thigh
knee
calf

ankle

6 Create the front crotch curve. Starting from the preferred waist and ending somewhere along the crotch depth line you drew in step 5, form a curve that equals the front crotch length measurement plus ¼-inch ease. A French curve is very handy here because it has ruled measurements, so you can measure and draw at once. Alternatively, form your measuring tape into a curve of the appropriate length in the space between the preferred waist and crotch depth lines, and freehand the curve. Again, you may not need the entire length of the crotch depth line, or you may need to add a little more length to the line to meet your curve. If you need to lower or raise the preferred waist point to generate a curve with the right measurement, that works too, though I like to start with modifying the length of the crotch depth line as described previously.

You'll want to experiment with this area, and in the end will probably adjust both the crotch depth line and the waist point. A lot of front lower body slopers are slightly lower (about 1 inch) at the center of the waist, but as with so much else, it's a matter of personal preference.

7 Connect the endpoints of the horizontal lines to form the pant leg. Smooth out any angles. Compare the inseam measurement you recorded against the sloper inseam. Since you want a little bit of ease, the numbers don't need to exactly match, but should be pretty close—within an inch, let's say. If the numbers are off by more than that, you may need to move the crotch curve position along the extended line to lengthen or shorten the inseam. Don't forget to redraw the upper crotch curve too; as mentioned in step 6, you might ultimately raise or lower the waistline to compensate for the shift.

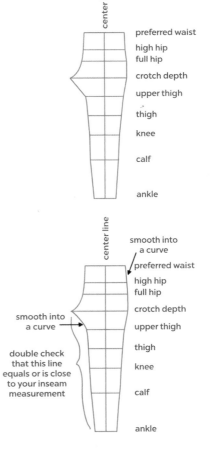

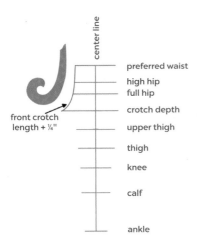

STEP 7

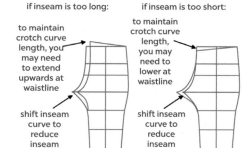

if inseam is too long:

to maintain crotch curve length, you may need to extend upwards at waistline

shift inseam curve to reduce inseam length

if inseam is too short:

to maintain crotch curve length, you may need to lower at waistline

shift inseam curve to reduce inseam length

8 Square corners (see page 72), add grain-line (see page 48) and label as "front lower body sloper," and cut out. We are not adding seam allowances at this time.

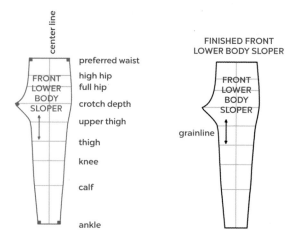

center line

FRONT LOWER BODY SLOPER

preferred waist

high hip
full hip

crotch depth

upper thigh

thigh

knee

calf

ankle

FINISHED FRONT LOWER BODY SLOPER

FRONT LOWER BODY SLOPER

grainline

BACK LOWER BODY SLOPER

This is basically the same process as the front lower body sloper, except the crotch curve will be deeper, a little bit more ease is added overall, and the waist will be raised at the center back. We won't be adding darts during the initial drafting of the back sloper but will do so during the muslin stage.

1 Draw a vertical line equal to the outseam measurement. This will be the center line for the back.

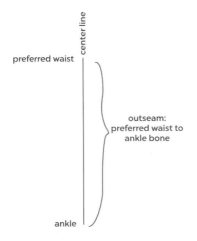

2 Plot vertical measurement points for preferred waist, high hip, full hip, crotch depth, thigh, knee, calf, and ankle. If using Swedish tracing paper, it might be easier to trace the vertical points of the front lower body sloper. You could also trace the horizontal lines of the front lower body sloper, but be aware that the measurements, curves, and ease will be different for the back. The back sloper is always bigger than the front.

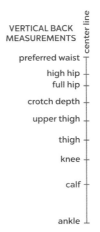

VERTICAL BACK
MEASUREMENTS

- preferred waist
- high hip
- full hip
- crotch depth
- upper thigh
- thigh
- knee
- calf
- ankle

3 Divide the following measurements by 2. The back preferred waist, high hip, and full hip are calculated by subtracting the front side-to-side measurements from the circumference.

Divide by 2:
- Back preferred waist
- Back high hip
- Back full hip
- Upper thigh circumference
- Thigh circumference
- Knee circumference
- Calf circumference
- Ankle circumference

Now add the ease to each:
- Preferred waist: ½ inch
- High hip: ¼ inch
- Full hip: ¼ inch
- Upper thigh: ½ inch
- Thigh: ½ inch
- Knee: ½ inch
- Calf: ½ inch
- Ankle: 1½ inches

4 Using the final measurements you calculated in step 3 (including the ease), draw horizontal lines centered on the vertical points. We will address the crotch depth in the next step.

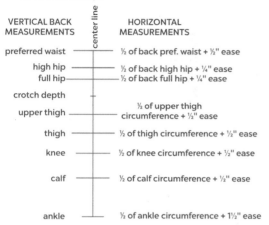

VERTICAL BACK MEASUREMENTS | center line | HORIZONTAL MEASUREMENTS

preferred waist — ½ of back pref. waist + ½" ease

high hip — ½ of back high hip + ¼" ease
full hip — ½ of back full hip + ¼" ease

crotch depth —

upper thigh — ½ of upper thigh circumference + ½" ease

thigh — ½ of thigh circumference + ½" ease

knee — ½ of knee circumference + ½" ease

calf — ½ of calf circumference + ½" ease

ankle — ½ of ankle circumference + 1½" ease

5 For the crotch depth line, draw a horizontal line equal in length to the full hip line, then extend the line to the right about 3 inches. As with the front sloper, you may not need to use the entire extension, or you may need to add more; it depends on your crotch length. This extension is to give you a starting point, and you'll finalize this line in step 7.

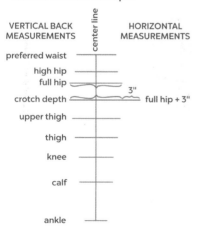

VERTICAL BACK MEASUREMENTS | center line | HORIZONTAL MEASUREMENTS

preferred waist —
high hip —
full hip —
crotch depth — full hip + 3"
upper thigh —
thigh —
knee —
calf —
ankle —

6 Raise the right side of the preferred waist point by about 1¼ inches and connect to the left outer edge of the preferred waist line, forming a line that angles up from left to right. Since our pants fabric pulls down when we sit, we need to add this extra bit here. The curvier you are, the more you may want to raise this preferred waist point.

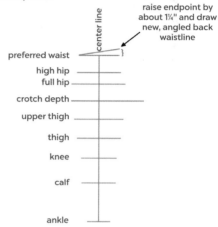

raise endpoint by about 1¼" and draw new, angled back waistline

center line

preferred waist —
high hip —
full hip —
crotch depth —
upper thigh —
thigh —
knee —
calf —
ankle —

7 Create back crotch curve. Starting from the preferred waist and ending somewhere along the crotch depth line from step 5, form a curve with a French curve or measuring tape that equals the back crotch length measurement plus ¼-inch ease. Again, you may not need the entire extended line for the crotch curve, or you may need to add a little more. If you need to lower or raise the preferred waist point to generate a curve with the right measurement, that's okay too. Just as you did with the front crotch curve, you'll want to experiment with this area.

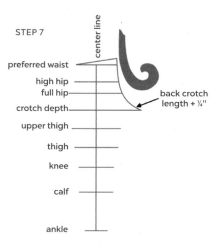

STEP 7

center line

preferred waist
high hip
full hip
crotch depth
upper thigh
thigh
knee
calf
ankle

back crotch length + ¼"

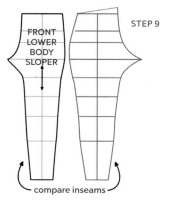

STEP 9

FRONT LOWER BODY SLOPER

compare inseams

if inseam is too long: if inseam is too short:

8 Connect the endpoints of the horizontal lines to form the pant leg. Smooth out any angles.

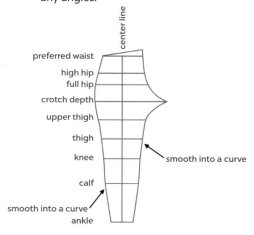

center line

preferred waist
high hip
full hip
crotch depth
upper thigh
thigh
knee
calf
ankle

smooth into a curve

smooth into a curve

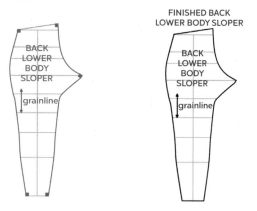

to maintain crotch curve length, you may need to extend upward at waistline

shift inseam curve to reduce inseam length

to maintain crotch curve length, you may need to lower at waistline

shift inseam curve to reduce inseam length

10 Square corners, add grainline, label as "back lower body sloper," and cut out. We are not adding seam allowances at this time.

BACK LOWER BODY SLOPER

grainline

FINISHED BACK LOWER BODY SLOPER

BACK LOWER BODY SLOPER

grainline

9 Align (see page 67) the front and back slopers to make sure both the outseams and inseams match up. The front and back inseams can be slightly different; the back inseam will most likely be a little bit longer, and you can stretch the front piece to match. However, if the difference is more than an inch, you might want to shift the crotch curve and may need to adjust the waist to maintain the measurements you need.

LOWER BODY SLOPER MUSLIN

1 Press your muslin or cotton fabric.

2 Place paper sloper patterns on the fabric and trace. Add ⅝-inch seam allowance (see page 67) as shown. You will cut two front pieces and two back pieces.

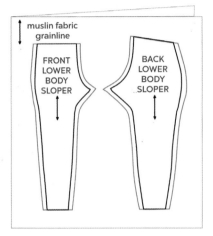

muslin fabric grainline

FRONT LOWER BODY SLOPER

BACK LOWER BODY SLOPER

3 With right sides facing, machine baste crotch curve of front pieces with a ⅝-inch seam allowance. Repeat for back pieces.

muslin front WS

muslin back WS

4 With right sides facing, machine baste the front and back together at inseam with a ⅝-inch seam allowance.

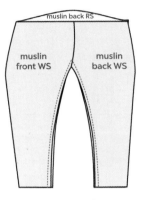

muslin back RS

muslin front WS

muslin back WS

5 With right sides facing, machine baste one side all the way from waist to hem. On the other side, start a few inches below the waist.

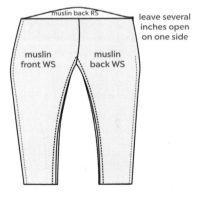

muslin back RS

muslin front WS

muslin back WS

leave several inches open on one side

6 Turn muslin right side out and try on. If there's excess fabric around your high hips and waist area at the front and/or back, pinch the excess fabric to shape darts and mark along pinched fabric with a Sharpie or pen to transfer onto your sloper. The dart apex should always point to the fullest part of your body for the best fit, and a dart length of about 3 inches is a nice starting point, which you'll probably want to adjust. See the darts (page 69) and transferring markings section (page 59) for more information.

Congrats! You've created your first slopers!

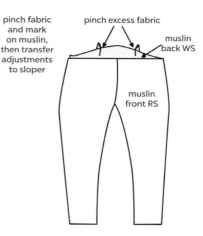

pinch fabric and mark on muslin, then transfer adjustments to sloper

pinch excess fabric

muslin back WS

muslin front RS

COMMON LOWER BODY SLOPER FIT ISSUES

How's the fit? The most challenging fit areas for the lower body sloper are usually around the crotch and hips, and the legs often twist due to the position and length of the inseam. For resources on additional fit issues see page 262.

CROCH/HIP FIT: The main issues with crotch/hip fit can fall into either too much bagginess or extra tightness. Remember, you want the sloper to be snug. Making small adjustments to the crotch curve and inseam will often resolve the issues.

TWISTING LEGS: Twisting legs result when the distribution of fabric isn't balanced between the front and back, usually at the inseam. To correct this, you will need to either add length or shorten the inseam as shown here.

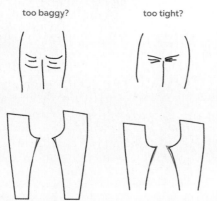

too baggy?

too tight?

try trimming crotch length and inseam

try adding to crotch length and inseam (you will need to tape extra paper)

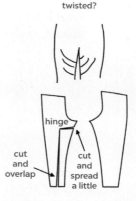

twisted?

hinge

cut and overlap

cut and spread a little

try lengthening the inseam of the side that is pulling a bit; if twisting toward the front, lenghten the front inseam and vice versa if pulling toward the back

the projects

Before You Begin . . .

- -

Please keep the following in mind as you try out your custom slopers:

- After you've drafted the patterns for the following projects, it's always a good idea to make a quick muslin out of fabric with a similar weight and drape as your "nice" fabric to assess the fit. I recommend using inexpensive fabrics for muslins, and old sheets/bedding are very useful. This saves time and effort for when you proceed to your final version.

- Always prepare fabrics before cutting or sewing with them by washing and pressing.

- Aligning and squaring: If you've completed the slopers section, you will be familiar with truing up, walking, and squaring pattern pieces (see pages 67 and 72). I'll be using these terms frequently in the project instructions as well, so I highly recommend you familiarize yourself with these concepts if this is all new for you. In the project instructions, corners that need to be squared will be indicated like this:

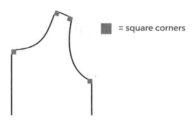

■ = square corners

- For information on adding seam allowances, see page 67. The aqua lines around pattern pieces depict the seam allowances and are meant to give you a quick visual reference on where to place them (they may not be drawn to scale).

- As for the yardage listed per project, they are based on my own size (I typically sew a size 12 or 14 in pattern clothing size and wear a size 6 or 8 in RTW, depending on the brand) so the actual required fabric will vary from person to person.
- In the construction section for each project, you will see a layout that looks something like this:

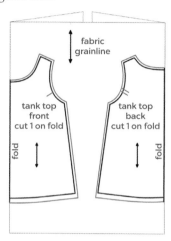

- You could absolutely lay out your pattern pieces as indicated, but the reason I included this is to show all the pattern pieces that will need to be cut out and when a pattern piece will be cut on the fold. Since the width of the fabric you'll be using may differ from the proportions in the illustration, please use this as a loose guide.
- I also want to note that while all of the following projects can be drafted from the slopers as the instructions show, you could also use what you already have. The measurements from a snug, well-fitting garment or favorite pattern could stand in for measurements from the slopers. And although I cite various measurements for extending hems, modifying necklines, and so on, it's important to be aware that the measurements cited in the projects are for my 5-foot 4-inch height, 39-inch bust, 32-inch waist, and 39-inch hips frame. The ultimate goal for these project instructions is for you to customize each and every one to *your* liking.

Happy sewing!

||||||||||||||||||||||||||||||||||||||||||||||||

TOPS

||||||||||||||||||||||||||||||||||||||||||||||||

TANK TOP

THIS WOVEN TANK IS A terrific basic pattern for launching into garment-making. Tank tops are so easy to sew up, and I can't imagine having too many. Enjoy experimenting with different hem lengths, necklines, and materials (for instructions on working with knits instead of wovens, see page 133).

SUPPLIES + MATERIALS

Drafting kit (see page 45)

Torso sloper (front and back)

Approx. 1½ yards woven
    fabric

Coordinating thread

FABRIC RECOMMENDATIONS

Cotton lawn, linen, chambray,
shirting, broadcloth

DRAFTING STEPS

1. Trace the slopers. Trace front and back slopers onto a separate piece of paper. Make sure to leave enough room around the traced pieces to make modifications and add seam allowances.

2. Make modifications to the traced slopers.

    a. Lower the front and back neckline. I lowered my front neckline by 3½ inches and the back neckline by 1½ inches. Using a French curve creates a nice smooth curve.

b. Reduce the shoulder width for both front and back for the tank top straps. To ensure my bra strap would be covered, I made mine about 2 inches wide, reducing about 1 inch on both the neck and shoulder sides.

c. Extend the hem horizontally by about 2 inches, then draw a straight line to connect the bottom of the armhole with the new hem width.

d. Square corners and curve hems (see page 72).

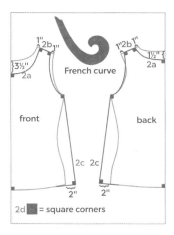

3 Align the pattern pieces and make adjustments as needed (see page 67). Cut out pattern pieces, leaving plenty of room to add seam allowances.

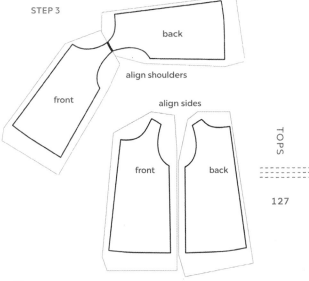

4 Measure neckline and armholes.

a. Place the pattern pieces with shoulders aligned and measure the neckline (front and back). Keep in mind that this is only half of the neckline, so you'll need to double it. Write down the full neckline measurement; I like to record it on the front pattern piece.

b. Get the measurement for the armhole as well and make a note of it. This will be the full armhole measurement.

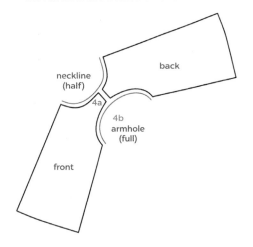

5. Add seam allowance as shown (see page 67). If you added a bust dart, fold the dart before adding seam allowances. Cut pattern pieces at seam allowance line, label, and add grainline (see page 48) and markings.

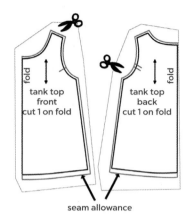

seam allowance

CONSTRUCTION STEPS

1. Place pattern pieces on fabric, trace, and cut out. If you added a bust dart, unfold the dart before tracing pattern.

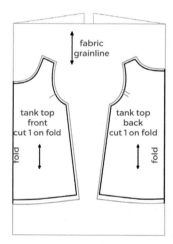

2. Draft neck and armhole bias facings directly on fabric based on the measurements you took. Bias facings are cut diagonal to the selvage (see page 47). Make the width 1¼ inches and use the measurements of the neckline and armhole for the length, respectively. We want the bias facings to be a little bit shorter than the neckline and armhole measurements, so we won't add any seam allowances to the length. Cut out. Optional: I don't usually press folded edges for the bias facings before attaching them, but it allows for more precision, so feel free to do so.

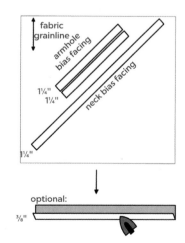

3 If applicable, sew darts (see page 69).

4 Sew shoulders. With right sides together, align shoulders of front and back pieces and sew with a ⅜-inch seam allowance. Finish raw edges and press seam allowance toward the back.

5 Sew sides with right sides facing and with a ⅜-inch seam allowance. Finish raw edges and press.

6 Attach neck bias facing.

a. Double-check that the bias facing fits snugly around the neckline first, and mark where to sew on the wrong side of the facing. Then stitch the facing along short ends with right sides together with a ⅜-inch seam allowance to form a loop. Trim seam allowance to ¼ inch and press open.

STEP 6A

b. With right sides of the top and bias facing together and aligning the facing seam at the center back, stitch ⅜ inch from the edge all the way around. Trim seam allowance to about ⅛ inch.

c. Press the raw, outer edge of the facing toward the wrong side by ⅜ inch, then fold and press it along the seam toward the wrong side of the top to enclose the seam allowance. Edgestitch along fold.

7 Repeat step 6 for armhole bias facings, making sure to line up the facing seam with the side seam at the bottom of the armhole.

back WS

front
RS

8 Sew hem. Fold hem by ⅜ inch toward the wrong side and press. Fold another ⅜ inch and press again. Starting at one of the sides, edgestitch along fold. Press and all done!

front
RS

back WS

double fold

Variation: Crop Tank or Long Tank

YOU CAN ACHIEVE A TOTALLY different vibe with just a quick hem change. You could, of course, determine a different hem length during drafting step 1, but here I show you how to alter the hem length once you have a pattern drafted (after drafting step 5). In order to preserve the squared corners and curve of the hem, make the modifications as described below.

MODIFICATIONS

- **To shorten:** Draw a horizontal line about halfway down the sloper for front and back pieces. Cut and overlap pieces by the amount you want to shorten the hem, making sure to match the changes on both pieces.

- Smooth out the side seam. If you don't want to cut apart the pattern piece, you could also fold it by half the amount desired and smooth out the side seam when you trace the modified pattern piece onto fabric.

TO SHORTEN STEP 2

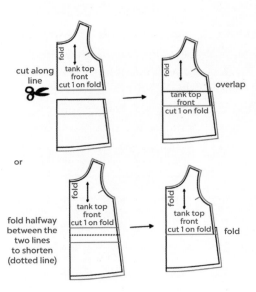

cut along line ✂

or

fold halfway between the two lines to shorten (dotted line)

fold

shorten and tape in place, then redraw the sides

- **To lengthen**: Draw a horizontal line for front and back pieces and cut apart in the same manner as if to shorten. Place a piece of paper as wide as each pattern piece underneath. Separate the cut pieces by the amount you want to lengthen the hem, with the extra paper underneath filling in the gap.
- Tape the spread pieces in place and smooth out the side seam.

cut to lengthen

lengthen and secure extra paper with tape and redraw sides

T-SHIRT

OVER THE YEARS, THE IDEAL T-shirt has been surprisingly elusive for me, even though it's such a simple garment. Now I've finally found it! I designed mine to be body skimming, but if you like your tees up close and personal, stretchy knit fabric allows you to have "negative ease" (see page 220), which means that the pattern pieces can be smaller than your body measurements and still fit comfortably. This version has a high-low hem, and a short, dressy cap sleeve. Of course, the beauty of patternmaking is that now you can customize it to be *your* perfect tee!

SUPPLIES + MATERIALS

Drafting kit (see page 45)

Torso sloper (front and back)

Sleeve sloper

Approx. 2 yards stretchy fabric

Ballpoint machine needle

Coordinating thread

Optional: stay tape

⊩⊩⊩⊩⊩⊩⊩⊩⊩⊩⊩⊩⊩⊩

FABRIC RECOMMENDATIONS

Bamboo knit, jersey, tencel, linen jersey

⊩⊩⊩⊩⊩⊩⊩⊩⊩⊩⊩⊩⊩⊩

Note: For knits, always use a ballpoint needle and a stretch-friendly stitch, such as a zigzag or knit-specific stretch stitch on your machine. My preference is to set my zigzag width to 2 millimeters and length to 2.5 millimeters. Alternatively, use a serger/overlocker if you have one. Since most knits don't fray, you don't need to finish raw edges, but feel free to do so if you like.

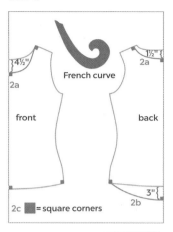

DRAFTING STEPS

1. Trace the slopers. If you added a bust dart for your sloper, fold and tape down before tracing, since you won't need darts for knits. Trace front sloper, back sloper, and the top portion of the sleeve sloper (sleeve cap and at least 2 inches) onto separate pieces of paper. (Two inches from the bottom of the bicep line forms a cap-style sleeve for me.) Make sure to leave enough space around the traced pieces to make modifications and add seam allowances.

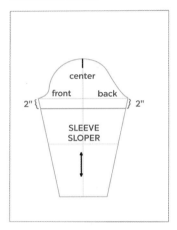

2. Make modifications to slopers.

   a. Lower front and back necklines. I lowered the front by 4½ inches for a deeper scoop and the back by 1½ inches. Using a French curve achieves a smooth curve.

   b. Extend the back hem vertically by about 3 inches from the center back line.

   c. Square corners and curve hems (see page 72) for front and back slopers, and square corners for sleeve.

STEP 2

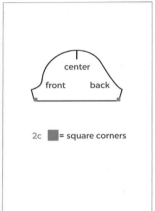

3. Align the pattern pieces and make adjustments as needed (see page 67). Cut out pattern pieces, leaving plenty of room to add seam allowances.

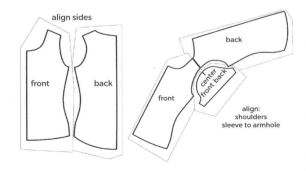

4 Place the pattern pieces with shoulders aligned and measure the neckline (front and back). Keep in mind that this is only half of the neckline, so you'll need to double it. Write down the full neckline measurement (I like to record it on the front pattern piece).

5 Add seam allowance as shown (see page 67). Cut pattern pieces at seam allowance, label, and add grainline (see page 48) and markings.

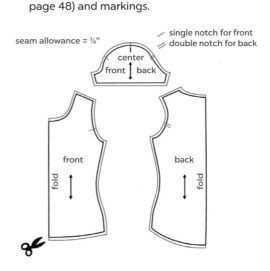

seam allowance = ⅜"

single notch for front
double notch for back

center
front | back

front

back

fold

fold

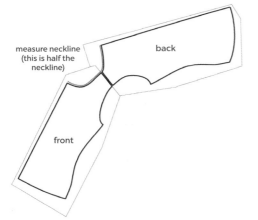

measure neckline (this is half the neckline)

back

front

CONSTRUCTION STEPS

1 Place pattern pieces on fabric, trace, and cut out.

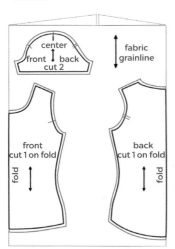

center
front | back
cut 2

fabric grainline

front
cut 1 on fold

back
cut 1 on fold

fold

fold

2 Make neckband. Draft neckband directly on fabric along the stretchiest part of the fabric, which for knits is typically cross-wise (perpendicular to the selvage). The neckband should be 1¼ inches wide and the length of the full neckline measurement. (We want the neckband to be a little bit shorter than the actual neckline, so we won't add any seam allowance to the length.) Cut out neckband.

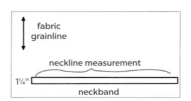

fabric grainline

neckline measurement

1¼"

neckband

3 Optional: iron stay tape along shoulder edges to prevent stretching.

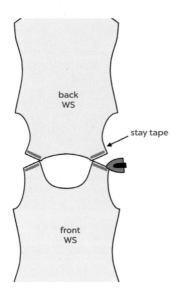

5 Attach sleeves. With right sides together and lining up the markings, attach sleeves with a ⅜-inch seam allowance. Finish raw edges if desired. Press seam allowances toward sleeve.

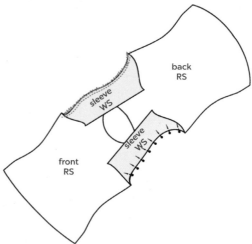

4 Sew shoulders. With right sides together, align shoulders of front and back pieces. Using a stretch or zigzag stitch, sew with a ⅜-inch seam allowance. Finish raw edges if desired. Press seam allowances toward back.

6 Sew sleeves and sides. With right sides together, sew the bottom of the sleeve all the way down the side, pivoting under the arm, with a ⅜-inch seam allowance. Repeat for other side. Finish raw edges if desired. Press seam allowances toward back.

7 Attach neckband.

a. Double-check that the length matches the neckline (see page 129). Remember that you want the neckband to be snug to avoid a gaping neckline. Then stitch along short ends with right sides together with a ⅜-inch seam allowance. Press seam allowance open.

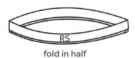

neckband

b. Fold the neckband in half lengthwise with wrong sides facing and press or steam lightly.

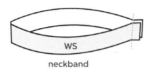

fold in half

c. Align raw edges with the neckband on the right side of the top (I like to put the seam at the center back), and sew ⅜ inch from the edge all the way around. Finish raw edges if desired. Press seam allowance away from neckband.

d. Topstitch about ⅛ inch from the seamline to secure seam allowance in place. You can use a long straight stitch or a narrow zigzag stitch for the topstitching.

8 Sew sleeve hems. Finish raw edge if desired. Fold hem by ⅜ inch toward the wrong side and press or lightly steam. Edgestitch. Repeat for other sleeve.

9 Repeat step 8 for the hem.

Variation: Long Sleeve Tee with Cuffs

TO MAKE THIS, WE JUST add long sleeves and cuffs to the T-shirt. The hem is straight and tuck-in-able, and a little more ease has been added by straightening the sides. Made out of French terry (my favorite!) or soft bamboo knit, this is ultimate loungewear. Comfy, comfy!

FABRIC RECOMMENDATIONS

Knit jersey, ponte knit, French terry (See note on page 133 for knit-specific tips.)

MODIFICATIONS

- In drafting step 1, I determined the length of the cuff I want with a ruler against my wrist and removed about 2½ inches from the bottom of the sleeve sloper.

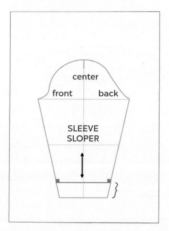

- In drafting step 2, straighten the sides, keeping the hem even.

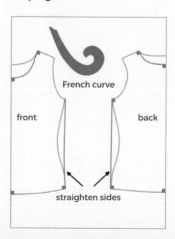

- Draft the sleeve cuff. Since I shortened the sleeve by 2½ inches and because the cuff will be folded in half, I made the cuff 5 inches high. The width is the same as the sleeve opening. You'll cut out two.

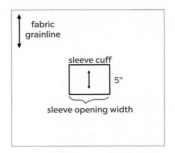

- Don't forget to add seam allowances as shown—we've got a few new ones—then cut pattern pieces at seam allowance, label, and add grainline (see page 48) and markings.

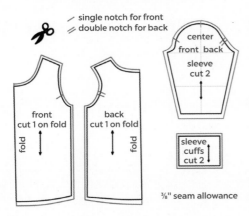

- Follow construction steps 1–7, then for step 8, attach the sleeve cuffs instead of hemming the sleeves. With right sides together, sew the short edges with a ⅜-inch seam allowance and fold in half with wrong sides facing. Align raw edges and sew the sleeve cuff to the sleeve opening with a ⅜-inch seam allowance. Finish raw edges if desired.

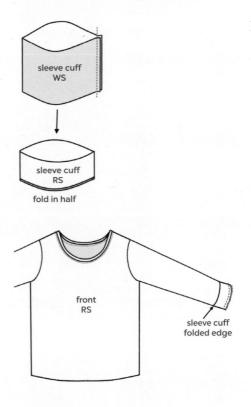

- Follow construction step 9 to hem the shirt.

V-NECK TOP

THIS TOP CAN EASILY GO from casual to dressy depending on the fabric you choose. You won't need the sleeve sloper for this project, since we will simply extend the torso sloper along the shoulder edges. Not only do you have fewer pattern pieces to manage, there's the added bonus of speeding up the sewing process! Try to find fabric that softly drapes; if the fabric is too stiff, it can easily start to look like hospital garb.

SUPPLIES + MATERIALS

Drafting kit (see page 45)

Torso sloper (front and back)

Approx. 2 yards woven fabric

Coordinating thread

FABRIC RECOMMENDATIONS

Cotton lawn, batiste, lightweight linen, linen/rayon blends

Note: if using zigzag stitches for finishing raw edges, go slowly with extra lightweight fabrics, as the feed dogs tend to eat them up.

DRAFTING STEPS

1. If you added a bust dart for your sloper, fold and tape down before tracing, since we'll be adding plenty of ease. Trace the front and back slopers onto a separate piece of paper. Make sure to leave enough space around the traced pieces to make modifications and add seam allowances.

2. Modify front sloper.

   a. Determine the position of the V-neck and mark on the center front. You can check an existing V-neck top that you like for reference, or drape your sloper on your body and mark a spot that feels good. I made my V-neck tip about 3½ inches above the bust apex. Then draw a diagonal line from the tip of the V to the neck/shoulder. Using the French curve (or freehand), curve this line ever so slightly away from the neck. This will help the neckline lie better on your body.

   b. Extend the shoulder and side into a kimono sleeve. I extended the sleeve 10½ inches from the outer shoulder point, following the slope of the shoulder. However, if the shoulder slope is quite steep, the sleeve won't drape as well and it may restrict arm movement, so consider extending the sleeve from the neck/shoulder point instead.

   c. Draw a vertical line from the top of the extended sleeve down to about 1½ inches below the armhole, and make sure that there is enough room for your arm to fit and for the sleeve to drape. Then draw a horizontal line for the bottom of the sleeve toward the side, but stop about 1 inch before the side.

STEP 1

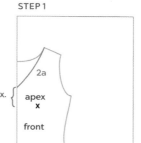

2a

approx. 3½"

apex
x

front

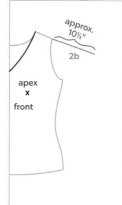

approx. 10½"

2b

apex
x

front

STEP 2A

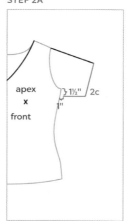

apex
x

front

1½"
1"
2c

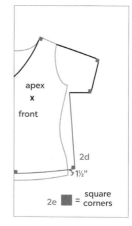

apex
x

front

2d
1½"

2e ■ = square corners

STEP 2B

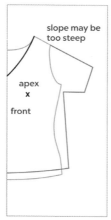

slope may be too steep

apex
x

front

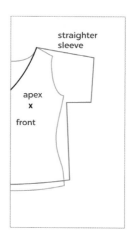

straighter sleeve

apex
x

front

d. Determine desired hem length and sweep (a.k.a. hem width)—I like to hold the sloper piece up to my body to eyeball it. Draw a corresponding horizontal line extending from the center line at desired hem length point. Connect the bottom of the sleeve to the hem. I made my hem about 1½ inches shorter than my sloper.

e. Square corners and curve hems (see page 72).

3 Modify back sloper.

a. If using tracing paper, place paper on top of the modified front piece and trace the shoulder, sleeve, side, and hem. Repeat steps b–e above for the back piece with the back sloper if using paper that isn't sheer.

b. Raise back neckline so it is basically a straight line—I raised mine by about 1¼ inches. You will be double-folding the fabric at the neckline, so you want to keep the curve on the flatter side. Curved edges are more challenging to fold evenly.

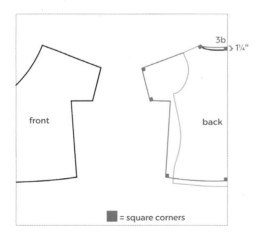

3b
↦ 1¼"

front   back

■ = square corners

4 Align the pattern pieces and make adjustments as needed (see page 67). Cut out pattern pieces, leaving plenty of room to add seam allowances.

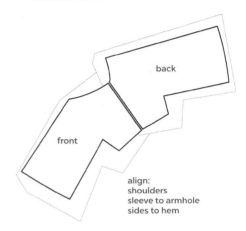

back

front

align:
shoulders
sleeve to armhole
sides to hem

5 Add seam allowances as shown (see page 67). Cut pattern pieces at seam allowance, label pattern pieces, and add grainline (see page 48) and markings.

seam allowance:
¾" for hem and sleeve hems
½" for neckline and front edge
⅜" for shoulders and sides

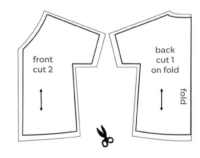

front
cut 2

back
cut 1
on fold

fold

CONSTRUCTION STEPS

1 Place pattern pieces on fabric, trace, and cut out.

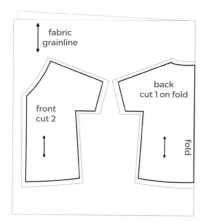

3 Finish raw edges of shoulder/sleeve for front and back pieces. Press.

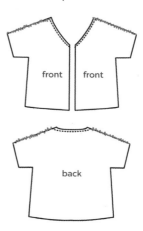

2 To stabilize the neckline, staystitch (see page 51) both front pieces along V-neck toward the center about ¼ inch from edge. Staystitch back neckline about ¼ inch from edge as well.

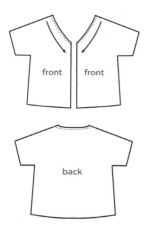

4 Sew shoulders. With right sides together, align shoulders of front and back pieces and sew with a ⅜-inch seam allowance. Press seam allowances open.

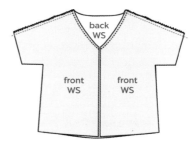

5 Sew sleeves and sides. With right sides facing and with a ⅜-inch seam allowance, making sure to pivot at the corner, sew the bottom of the sleeve and down the side to the hem. Repeat for other side. It's a good idea to reinforce these corners by shortening your stitches to about 2 millimeters. Clip into corners (careful not to cut into the seam!). Finish raw edges. Press seam allowance toward back.

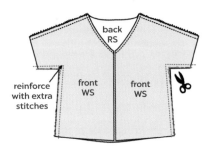

reinforce with extra stitches

back RS

front WS

front WS

6 Sew neckline. Fold neckline toward the wrong side by ¼ inch and press. Fold another ¼ inch and press. Edgestitch. The fabric may get a little fiddly and bunch up as you sew around the neckline, so use lots of pins to hold the folded edges in place, and smooth the fabric out as you stitch slowly.

7 Sew center front French seam. With *wrong sides* together, sew center front with a ¼-inch seam allowance. Trim the seam allowance to about ⅛ inch. Fold with right sides facing to encase the raw edges and press. Sew ¼ inch from folded edge. Presto, you have now created a French seam! Press the French seam to one side.

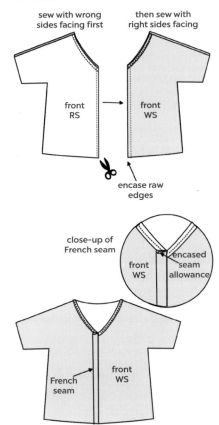

sew with wrong sides facing first

then sew with right sides facing

front RS

front WS

encase raw edges

close-up of French seam

encased seam allowance

front WS

French seam

front WS

8 Sew sleeve hems. Press sleeve edge toward wrong side by ⅜ inch. Fold another ⅜ inch and press. Edgestitch along fold. Repeat for other sleeve.

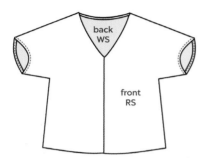

9 Repeat step 8 for the hem.

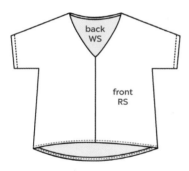

Variation: Button-Down V-Neck Top

IT'S EASY TO CHANGE THE look of the V-neck top in a big way. All you need to do is extend the center front, then sew buttonholes and buttons. You could also extend the sleeves even more—sewn in a heavier weight fabric like wool, this would make a sweet jacket.

MODIFICATIONS

- In drafting step 2, extend center front by 1½ inches.

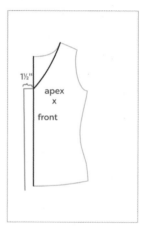

- In construction step 7, instead of creating the French seam, fold center front toward wrong side by ⅝ inch and press. Fold ⅝ inch again and press. Edgestitch in place. Repeat for other front piece.

EXTRA SUPPLIES + MATERIALS

½-inch buttons—as needed (I used 8)

Buttonhole foot

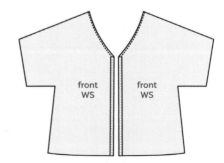

- Measure out buttonhole placement
  positions and mark along placket (the
  right placket is typical for women's
  tops, but you can choose whichever
  side you like). To prevent awkward
  gaping, place the first button at the
  fullest part of the bust and space out
  the other buttons evenly from there,
  making sure the top button is about
  ⅜ inch below the V point. Sew buttonholes using a buttonhole foot, then
  slice open with seam ripper. Overlap
  the front with the buttonhole placket
  on top and mark button positions
  inside each hole on the other placket.
  Sew on buttons.

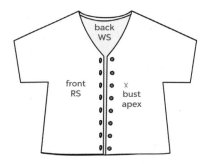

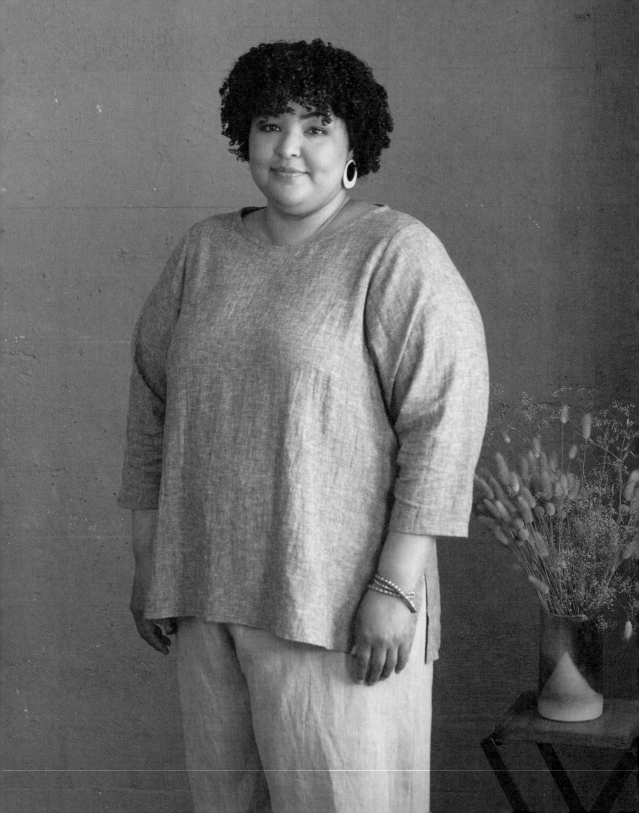

BATEAU TOP

SO VERY FRENCH, *NON*? THIS classic top incorporates some subtle shaping with darts. Don't worry—adding darts isn't all that difficult, and this is a looser-fitting top—so even if you don't get it exactly on point (ha) the first time, you'll still get some shaping. If you've already added a dart to your torso sloper, just simply trace the sloper and skip the dart section.

SUPPLIES + MATERIALS

Drafting kit (see page 45)

Torso sloper (front and back)

Sleeve sloper

Approx. 2¼ yards woven fabric

Coordinating thread

Optional: awl

FABRIC RECOMMENDATIONS

Cotton (cotton lawn is especially nice), linen, linen/rayon blends

DRAFTING STEPS

1. Trace the front, back, and sleeve slopers onto a separate piece of paper. Make sure to leave enough space around the traced pieces to make modifications and add seam allowances.

2 Modify front sloper.

a. Create the boat neck. On the traced front piece, make the neckline shallower and wider, using a French curve. I started by reducing the shoulder width by 2 inches on the neck side. (If you wear a bra, you can check whether your strap will show by placing the paper along your shoulder.) Then I raised the center point of the neckline by ½ inch to make the curve shallower to sit right around the hollow of my neck. Connect the center point and new shoulder width.

b. Extend the bottom of the armhole horizontally by ½ inch.

c. Draw a horizontal line from the bottom center front to about 1 inch past the hip, and connect the end of this line to the new armhole bottom from the previous step.

d. Square corners (see page 72).

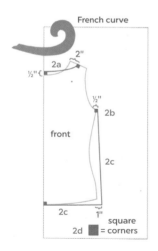

3 Repeat step 2 for the back sloper, but lower the neckline by about ¼ inch.

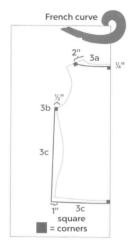

4 Modify sleeve sloper. Add ½ inch on each side of the sleeve. Then shorten the sleeve to ¾ length. For my sleeve, I shortened it 6 inches. A ¾-length sleeve typically is about 3 inches past the elbow. Connect the points to make new sides.

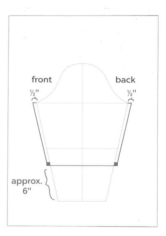

5 Add darts to front piece (see page 87).

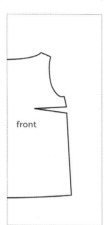

front

6 Square corners and curve hems (see page 72).

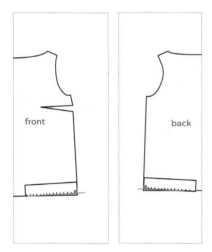

front   back

7 Determine where you would like the side slit to start, and mark on both front and back. I marked mine 3 inches from the bottom edge.

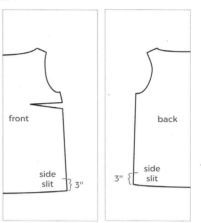

front   back

side slit   } 3"   3" { side slit

8 Align the pattern pieces and make adjustments as needed (see page 67). Fold the dart downward and tape in place to check alignment. Cut out pattern pieces, leaving plenty of room to add seam allowances.

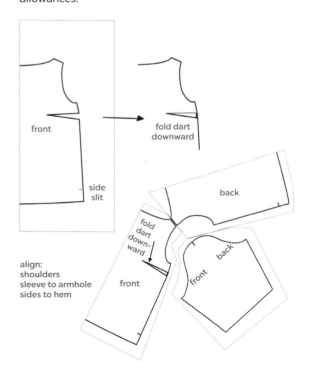

front   fold dart downward

back

side slit

fold dart downward

align:
shoulders
sleeve to armhole
sides to hem

front   front   back

9 Place the pattern pieces with shoulders aligned and measure the neckline (front and back). Keep in mind that this is only half of the neckline, so you'll need to double it. Write down the full neckline measurement (I like to record it on the front pattern piece).

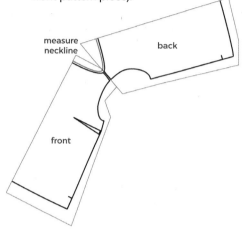

measure neckline

back

front

10 Add seam allowances as shown (see page 67). Cut pattern pieces at seam allowance, label, and add grainline (see page 48) and markings. For the dart section, fold it as if you're sewing it with the dart pointing downward, then cut to seam allowance line.

/ single notch for front
// double notch for back

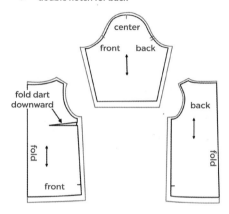

center

front   back

fold dart downward

fold

front

back

fold

seam allowance:
¾" for hem and sleeve hems
½" for sides of sleeves
½" for sides of front and back
⅜" for everything else

CONSTRUCTION STEPS

1 Place pattern pieces on fabric, trace, and cut out. Tip: using an awl to poke a hole through the fabric to mark the dart apex helps when pressing the darts.

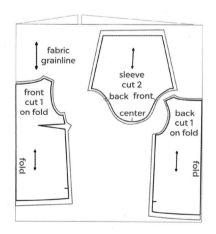

fabric grainline

front
cut 1
on fold

sleeve
cut 2
back front

center

back
cut 1
on fold

fold

fold

2 Draft the neck bias facing directly on the fabric, based on the full neckline measurement from drafting step 9. The facing should be 1¼ inches wide and the length of the full neckline measurement (we want the neck bias facing to be a little bit shorter than the actual neckline, so we won't add any seam allowance to the length). Cut out. Optional: I don't usually press folded edges for the bias strips before attaching them, but it allows for more precision, so feel free to do so.

STEP 2

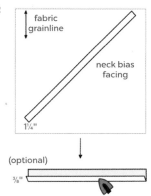

fabric grainline

neck bias facing

1¼"

(optional)

⅜"

③ Sew darts (see page 69).

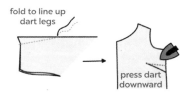

fold to line up dart legs

press dart downward

④ Sew shoulders. With right sides together, align shoulders of front and back pieces and sew with a ⅜-inch seam allowance. Finish raw edges. Press seam allowances toward back.

front WS

⑤ Attach sleeves. With right sides together and lining up the markings, attach sleeve to armhole with a ⅜-inch seam allowance. Make sure to distribute the sleeve cap as evenly as possible along the armhole. Finish raw edges and press seam allowance toward sleeve. Repeat for other sleeve.

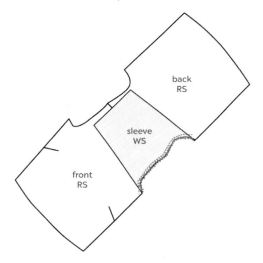

back RS

sleeve WS

front RS

⑥ Sew sleeves and sides. With right sides together, sew the bottom of the sleeve, pivot under the arm, and continue down the side with a ½-inch seam allowance, stopping at the slit marking. Repeat for other side. Finish raw edges up to the slit markings and press.

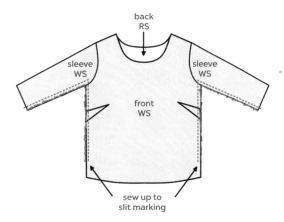

back RS

sleeve WS

sleeve WS

front WS

sew up to slit marking

7 Sew side slits. Fold and press raw edges of the slits toward the wrong side by ¼ inch twice. Edgestitch. Because the folded edges are quite narrow, stitch slowly to prevent the fabric from shifting around.

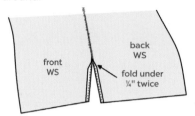

front
WS

back
WS

fold under
¼" twice

8 Attach neck bias facing.

a. Double-check that the bias facing fits snugly around the neckline first (see page 129), then stitch along short ends with right sides together with a ¼-inch seam allowance. Press seam allowance open.

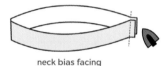

neck bias facing

b. Then with right sides of the top and bias facing together and aligning the facing seam at the center back, stitch ⅜ inch from the edge all the way around. Trim seam allowance to about ⅛ inch.

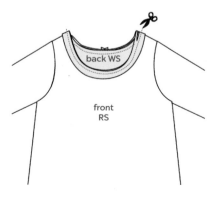

back WS

front
RS

c. Press the outer edge of the facing toward the wrong sides by ⅜ inch to enclose the raw edge, then fold and press along the seam toward the wrong side of the top. Edgestitch along fold.

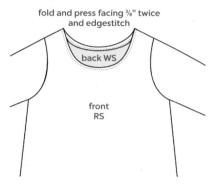

fold and press facing ⅜" twice
and edgestitch

back WS

front
RS

9 Sew sleeve hems. Fold sleeve edge by ⅜ inch toward the wrong side and press. Fold another ⅜ inch and press again. Edgestitch along fold. Press. Repeat for other sleeve.

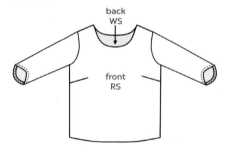

back
WS

front
RS

10 Repeat step 9 for the hem and all done!

front
RS

back WS

Variation: Woven Tee

TAKE AWAY THE SLEEVES, DARTS, and slits, and you're left with the easiest possible woven tee. Roomy yet stylish, this pattern shines when sewn in linen or soft cotton. For this variation, you will not need the sleeve sloper and will extend the shoulder; the Knit Cap Sleeve Dress (page 165) has a similar shape and technique, but since this is a woven top, we will be modifying the Bateau Top instructions.

- In drafting steps 1b and 2b: Extend underarm horizontally by an extra ¾ inch for front and back.
- In drafting steps 1c and 2c: Extend hem sweep (or width) an additional 1 inch, a total extension of 2 inches for me.
- Additionally, make the following modifications for both front and back:
  a. Slightly curve waist, following the silhouette of the sloper.
  b. Extend shoulder width to create sleeve (see page 141). I extended mine by 5 inches.
  c. Add a ⅜-inch seam allowance all around.
- Follow the construction steps, but skip the darts and slits.

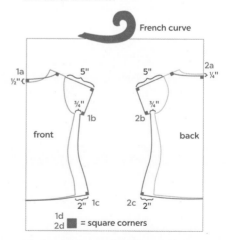

French curve

MODIFICATIONS

- In drafting steps 1a and 1b: Make the neckline shallower and wider using a French curve. I reduced the shoulder width by 2 inches on the neck side, raised the center point of the front neckline by ½ inch, and lowered the back neckline by ¼ inch. Connect the center point and new shoulder width.

DRESSES + TUNICS

SLEEVELESS DRESS WITH POCKETS

YOU'LL FIND YOURSELF REACHING FOR this comfy dress as often on summery beach days as on relaxed days at home; it's a dream in breezy linen. I made mine closer to a maxi length, but you can customize it to any length you like. The pockets add utilitarianism here, and the bias tapes for the neckline and armhole are designed to be visible on the right side of the dress, unlike the bias facings for other projects like the Tank Top or Bateau Top.

SUPPLIES + MATERIALS

Drafting kit (see page 45)

Torso sloper (front and back)

Approx. 3 yards woven fabric

Coordinating thread

⊓⊓⊓⊓⊓⊓⊓⊓⊓⊓⊓⊓⊓⊓⊓⊓⊓⊓⊓⊓⊓

FABRIC RECOMMENDATIONS

Cotton lawn, linen, linen blends, chambray, shirting, broadcloth

DRAFTING STEPS

1. Trace the front and back slopers onto a separate piece of paper. Make sure to leave enough space around the traced pieces to make modifications and add seam allowances.

sewing love

2 Modify the slopers.

a. Lower the neckline. I lowered the front by about 3 inches and the back by about 1½ inches from the center neckline.

b. Reduce the shoulder width for both front and back. I made mine about 2 inches wide, reducing more on the neck side than the shoulder side. Connect new shoulders to make new neckline and arm-holes. A French curve is useful for this.

c. Lengthen hem. I measured the distance from where the bottom of my sloper hits to just past my calves and extended my hem by 14 inches (I'm 5 feet, 4 inches tall).

d. Determine the hem width. Extend hem to desired width (I added about 8 inches from the bottom corner of the sloper, making the hem line about 18 inches from the center) and connect to bottom of armhole, gently sloping the side along the waist area.

e. Square corners and curve hems (see page 72).

STEP 2

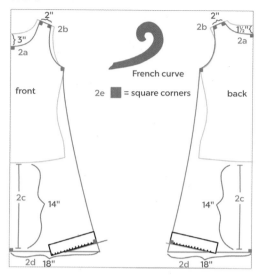

3 Use the template provided for the pocket on page 259. Trace the template and cut it out. A ⅜-inch seam allowance is included.

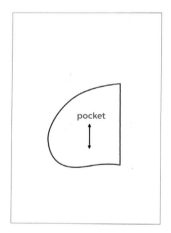

4 Align the pattern pieces and make adjustments as needed (see page 67). Leaving plenty of room to add seam allowances later, cut out pattern pieces.

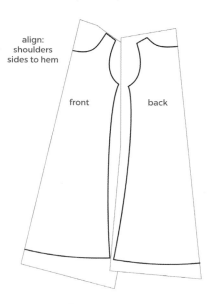

align:
shoulders
sides to hem

front   back

6 Add seam allowance as shown (see page 67). If you added a bust dart, fold the dart before adding seam allowances. Cut pattern pieces at seam allowance, label, and add grainline (see page 48) and markings. Make sure to mark the pocket positions on both front and back pieces. To determine the pocket positions, I drape the drafted pattern pieces on my body and pretend to stick my hand in a pocket and mark the spot on the front pattern piece, then match it on the back.

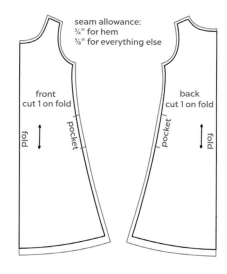

seam allowance:
¾" for hem
⅜" for everything else

front
cut 1 on fold

fold

pocket

back
cut 1 on fold

pocket

fold

5 Measure neckline and armholes.

a. Place the pattern pieces with shoulders aligned and measure the neckline (front and back). Keep in mind that this is only half of the neckline, so you'll need to double it. Write down the full neckline measurement (I like to record it on the front pattern piece).

b. Take and record the measurement for the armhole as well. This will be the full armhole measurement.

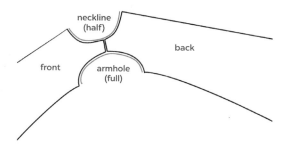

neckline
(half)

back

front   armhole
(full)

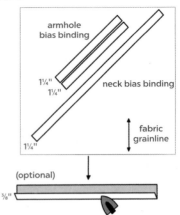

CONSTRUCTION STEPS

1. If applicable, unfold dart. Place pattern pieces on fabric, trace, and cut out. A ⅜-inch seam allowance is already incorporated into the pocket template.

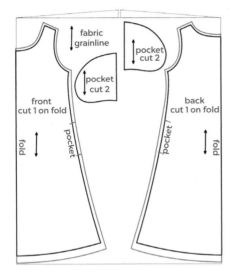

front cut 1 on fold

fabric grainline

pocket cut 2

pocket cut 2

back cut 1 on fold

fold

pocket

pocket

fold

2. Draft the bindings. Draft neck and armhole bias bindings directly on the fabric based on the measurements from step 5 of the drafting section. I made my binding 1¼ inches wide and used the measurement of the neckline for the length; armhole bindings should be 1¼ inches wide and the same length as the armholes. We want the bias facings to be a little bit shorter than the actual neckline and armholes so we won't add any seam allowance to the length. Cut out. Optional: I don't usually press folded edges for the bias strips before attaching them, but it allows for more precision so feel free to do so.

STEP 2

armhole bias binding

1¼"
1¼"

neck bias binding

fabric grainline

1¼"

(optional)

⅜"

3. If applicable, sew darts (see page 69).

4. Attach pockets. With right sides together, pin one set of pockets and front piece together at markings and sew along the straight edge with a ⅜-inch seam allowance. Repeat for back piece and other set of pockets. Finish raw edges and press pockets away from dress. Understitch seam allowance to the pockets about ⅛ inch from seam (see page 51).

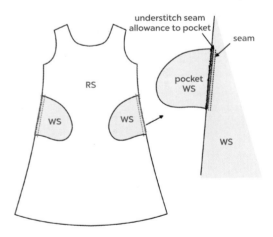

understitch seam allowance to pocket

seam

RS

pocket WS

WS

WS

WS

5 Sew shoulders. With right sides together, align shoulders of front and back pieces and sew with a ⅜-inch seam allowance. Finish raw edges and press seam allowance toward back.

6 Sew sides and pockets. Sew sides of main front and back pieces, pivoting at the top corner of the pocket and sewing around the pocket bag with a ⅜-inch seam allowance, then pivot at the bottom of the pocket and continue sewing down the side to the hem. Finish raw edges and press.

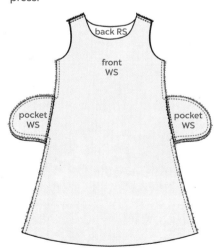

7 Attach neck bias binding.

a. Double-check that the bias binding fits snugly around the neckline first (see page 129) and mark where to sew. Then stitch along short ends with right sides together. Trim seam allowance to ¼ inch and press open.

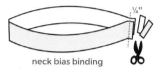

neck bias binding

b. With the wrong side of the dress and the right side of the bias binding together and starting at the center back, stitch ⅜ inch from the edge all the way around. Trim seam allowance to about ⅛ inch.

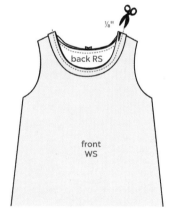

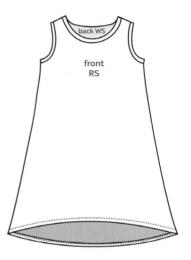

c. Press the outer edge of the binding toward the wrong side by ⅜ inch to encase the seam allowance, then fold and press along the seam toward the right side of the dress. Edgestitch along fold.

9 Sew hem. Fold hem by ⅜ inch toward wrong side and press. Fold another ⅜ inch and press again. Edgestitch along fold. Press and all done!

8 Sew armhole bias bindings. Repeat step 7 for armhole bias bindings, making sure to line up binding seam at the bottom of the armhole.

Variation: V-Neck Sleeveless Dress

THE V-NECK TOP (SEE PAGE 140) uses an easy method to create the V-neck, but it requires a center seam and sometimes that's not the design you want. Enter the V-neck bias tape method. This technique yields a clean, professional finish, and I just love the origami-like step of wrapping one end of the bias tape around the other.

Note: in construction step 6, you may want to follow the directions as given so the bias tape will be visible, or you can sew it as a facing that matches the V-neckline but will not be visible from the front (see Tank Top, page 125).

MODIFICATIONS

- In drafting step 2, draw the V-neck for the front pattern piece (see V-Neck Top, page 140).

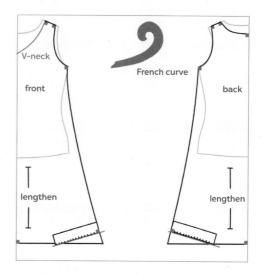

- In construction step 2, make sure to add at least 3 extra inches to the length when drafting the neck bias binding.

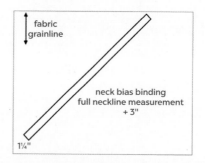

- In construction step 6, attach the bias tape this way instead:

  a. Staystitch (see page 51) the neckline.

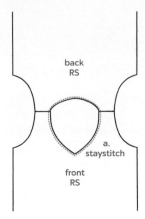

back
RS

a.
staystitch

front
RS

b. With right sides together and aligning raw edges, pin the bias tape all around the neckline, starting at the point of the V. Sew along the neckline with a ⅜-inch seam allowance, moving the overhanging part of the bias tape as you get to the other side of the V.

c. Except where the bias tape overlaps, trim seam allowance to about ¼ inch all around the neckline. Then clip into the seam allowance as close to the point of the V as you can.

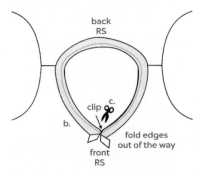

back
RS

clip c.

b.

fold edges
out of the way

front
RS

d. Flip the bias tape to the wrong side to enclose the raw edges; the two ends should overlap. Fold the raw edges of the overlapping bias tape and press along entire bias tape.

e. Wrap one end of the bias tape around the other end and pin to secure. Trim the raw edge that is sticking out. Edgestitch along fold, pivoting at the V point.

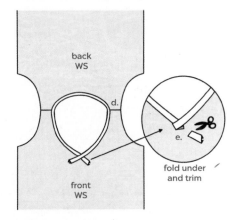

back
WS

d.

e.

fold under
and trim

front
WS

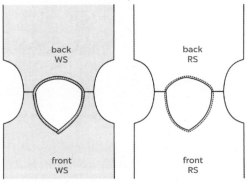

back
WS

front
WS

back
RS

front
RS

KNIT CAP SLEEVE DRESS

THIS DRESS IS BASICALLY A tee shirt: synonymous with supreme comfort.
Unless you want a very clingy fit, select a knit with good recovery that's slightly
thicker, like ponte. Since it's just two pieces and a neckband, it's a super-fast sew!

SUPPLIES + MATERIALS

Drafting kit (see page 45)

Torso sloper (front and back)

Approx. 2 yards stretchy fabric

Ballpoint machine needle

Coordinating thread

ıııııııııııııııııııııııı

FABRIC RECOMMENDATIONS

Bamboo knit, medium-weight
jersey, tencel, ponte knit (See
note on page 133 for knit-
specific tips.)

DRAFTING STEPS

1. If you added a bust dart for your sloper,
fold and tape down before tracing, since
you won't need darts for knits. Trace the
front and back slopers onto a separate piece of paper. Make sure to leave
enough space around the traced pieces
to make modifications and add seam
allowances.

2 Modify slopers.

a. Lower neckline on front piece. I made mine 1 inch lower. Connect to neck/shoulder point. Using a French curve achieves a smooth curve.

b. Extend shoulders into a cap sleeve for both front and back. I added 4 inches.

c. Extend a perpendicular, horizontal line from bottom of armhole out to the side for about ¾–1 inch on front and back. Connect b to c.

d. Lengthen the front and back pattern pieces to desired hem length. I measured from where the bottom of the sloper hits to just a little past my knees, and I lengthened my hem by 12 inches.

e. Draw a perpendicular, horizontal line from the center to extend the skirt sweep (a.k.a. hem width) to desired width on front and back. I made the new hem 2 inches wider than the sloper hem. Connect bottom of armhole to new hem.

f. Curve the sides. I prefer to maintain a slight curve that follows the sloper silhouette to give the dress some shaping.

g. Square corners and curve hems (see page 72).

STEP 2

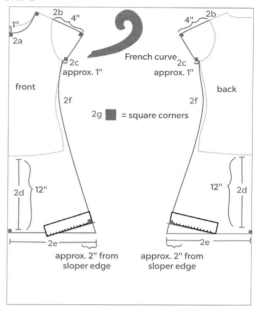

front

back

French curve

2g ■ = square corners

approx. 2" from sloper edge

approx. 2" from sloper edge

3 Align the pattern pieces and make adjustments as needed (see page 67). Cut out pattern pieces, leaving plenty of room to add seam allowances.

align:
shoulders
sleeve openings
sides to hem

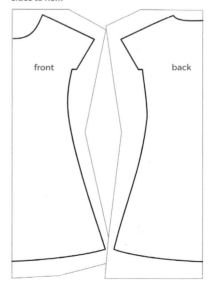

front

back

4 Place the pattern pieces with shoulders aligned and measure the neckline (front and back). Keep in mind that this is only half of the neckline, so you'll need to double it. Write down the full neckline measurement (I like to record it on the front pattern piece).

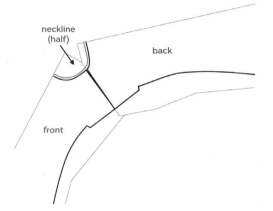

5 Add seam allowance as shown (see page 67). Cut pattern pieces at seam allowance, label, and add grainline (see page 48) and markings.

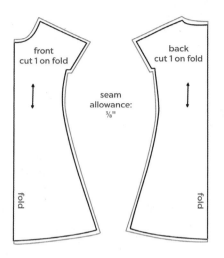

CONSTRUCTION STEPS

1 Place pattern pieces on fabric, trace, and cut out.

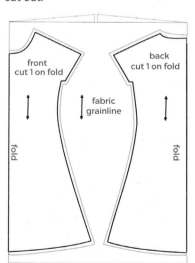

2 Make neckband. Draft neckband directly along the stretchiest part of the fabric, which for knits is typically crosswise (perpendicular to the selvage). The neckband should be 1¼ inches wide and the length of the full neckline measurement. (We want the neckband to be a little bit shorter than the actual neckline, so we won't add any seam allowance to the length.) Cut out neckband.

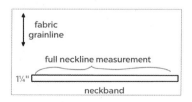

3 Sew shoulders. With right sides together, align shoulders of front and back pieces and sew with a ⅜-inch seam allowance. Finish raw edges if desired.

4 Sew sides. With right sides together, sew one side. Repeat for other side. Finish raw edges if desired.

5 Attach neckband.

a. Double-check that the length matches the neckline (see page 129), then stitch along short ends with right sides together with a ⅜-inch seam allowance. Press seam allowance open.

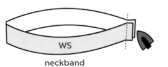

neckband

b. Fold the neckband in half lengthwise with wrong sides facing, and press or steam lightly.

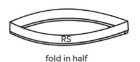

fold in half

c. Align raw edges with the neckband on the right side of the dress. I like to put the seam at the center back (some people prefer it at one of the shoulder seams), and sew ⅜ inch from the edge all the way around. Finish raw edges if desired.

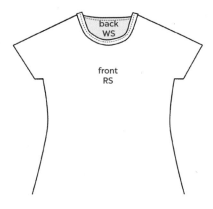

d. Topstitch about ⅛ inch from the neckline seamline on the right side of the dress to secure seam allowance in place. You can use a long straight stitch or a narrow zigzag stitch for the topstitch.

7 Repeat step 6 for the hem. That's it!

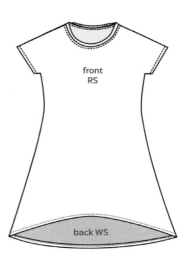

6 Sew sleeve hems. Finish raw edge if desired. Fold hem by ⅜ inch toward the wrong side and press or lightly steam. Edgestitch. Repeat for other sleeve.

Variation: Racerback Tank Dress

TO TRANSFORM THE DRESS INTO a sporty racerback style, all you need are two quick adjustments: instead of sleeves, draft racerback curves and finish them with armhole bands.

MODIFICATIONS

- In drafting step 2, modify armholes as shown.

    a. Reduce shoulder width about 1½ inches from outer shoulder edge side.

    b. On the back piece, draw a curved racerback, forming an angled J shape. Don't worry too much about the curve shape, though I do recommend keeping at least 3 inches between the center back and the deepest part of the arc. Otherwise, things might get floppy and unstable back there, but if that's the look you want, go for it.

    c. Bring in the side at the bottom of the armhole by about ½ inch to prevent gaping.

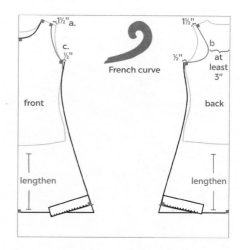

- In drafting step 4, measure the full armhole and draft armhole bands based on measurement. Make the width 1¼ inches, and the length should match the armhole measurement, like the neckband. No need to add seam allowance.

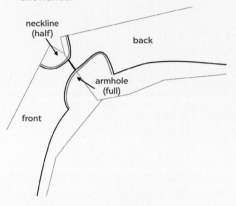

neckline (half)

back

armhole (full)

front

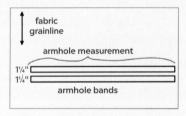

fabric grainline

armhole measurement

1¼"
1¼"

armhole bands

- Repeat construction step 5 (for neckband) to attach armhole bands, aligning the armhole band seam at the side seam.

front WS

back RS

KNIT COCOON TUNIC DRESS

JUST AS THE NAME SUGGESTS, this roomy tunic/dress will envelop you in warmth. The slightly curved silhouette keeps it from feeling sloppily oversized, and the cozy turtleneck and 3/4 sleeves balance out the generous proportions. The best part? You'll use the same pattern piece for both the front and back, which cuts the drafting time way down!

SUPPLIES + MATERIALS

Drafting kit (see page 45)

Torso sloper (front only)

Approx. 2 yards stretchy fabric

Ballpoint machine needle

Coordinating thread

FABRIC RECOMMENDATIONS

Bamboo knit, jersey, tencel, ponte knit, sweater knit, textured knits (See note on page 133 for knit-specific tips.)

DRAFTING STEPS

1 Note: we are going to use the same pattern piece for both the front and back. If you added a bust dart for your sloper, fold and tape down before tracing, as you won't need darts for knits. Trace the front sloper onto a separate piece of paper. Make sure to leave enough room around the traced piece to make modifications and add seam allowances.

2 Modify sloper.

a. Raise neckline by ½ inch. Measure and record new neckline length (I like to write it on the pattern piece). Keep in mind that this is ¼ of the neckline, so you will need to multiply it by 4 to get the full neckline length. Optional: if the neckline feels a little too low for the back, raise it another ½ inch when tracing the back piece on the fabric during the construction phase.

b. Extend shoulder by about 8 inches. I measured from my outer shoulder to about the middle of my upper arm.

c. Draw a vertical line down from the new shoulder endpoint that will be large enough to fit your arm and elbow with a couple extra inches of ease. I made my line 5½ inches. This is where the sleeve will be attached.

d. Draw a perpendicular, horizontal line toward the center from 2c.

e. Lengthen the hem by about 6 inches.

f. Extend the hem width about 3 inches and draw a line upward to connect to the bottom of the sleeve, curving the line slightly in a convex arc to create the cocoon silhouette. This will be the side.

g. Curve the line under the arm in a slight concave arc.

h. Square corners (see page 72).

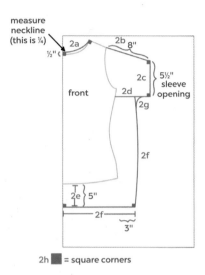

2h ■ = square corners

3 Draft the sleeves. To determine sleeve height, I measured from about the middle of my upper arm to about the middle of my forearm, which came out to 6½ inches. Using the sleeve opening measurement from step 2c and the sleeve length, draft as shown. Alternatively, this can be done directly on the fabric if you prefer.

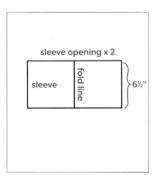

4 Draft the turtleneck with the width based on the full neckline measurement. I made the height 15 inches (just under 7½ inches when finished), and the turtleneck sits a touch under my chin. This will be folded in half; adjust the height to your preference.

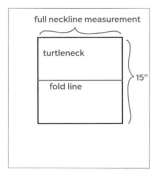

5 Align the pattern pieces and make adjustments as needed (see page 67). Cut out pattern pieces, leaving plenty of room to add seam allowances.

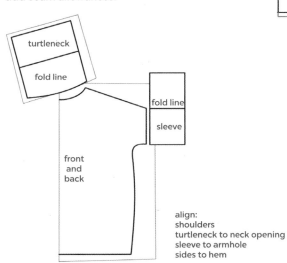

align:
shoulders
turtleneck to neck opening
sleeve to armhole
sides to hem

6 Add seam allowance as shown (see page 67). Cut pattern pieces at seam allowance, label, and add grainline (see page 48) and markings. Mark the center on the front and back tunic piece, and add a center front marking on the turtleneck piece to make attachment easier later (we'll want the turtleneck seam at the center back, and the notch will help match evenly to the center front).

seam allowance: ⅜"

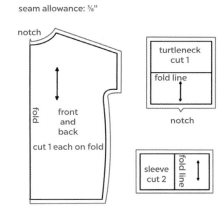

CONSTRUCTION STEPS

1 Place pattern pieces on fabric, trace, and cut out.

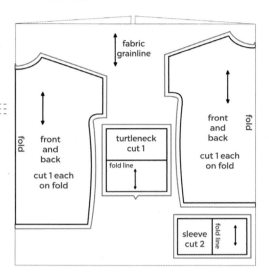

2 Sew shoulders. With right sides together, align shoulders of front and back pieces and sew with a ⅜-inch seam allowance. Finish raw edges if desired.

3 Attach sleeves. With right sides together and lining up the markings, attach sleeves with a ⅜-inch seam allowance. Finish raw edges if desired.

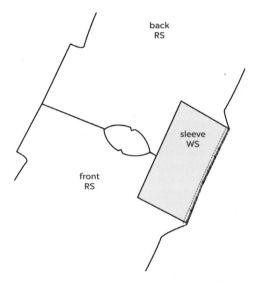

4 Sew sleeves and sides. With right sides together, sew the bottom of the sleeve down the side with a ⅜-inch seam allowance. Repeat for other side. Finish raw edges if desired. Leave top inside out to attach turtleneck in next step.

5 Sew the turtleneck.

a. With right sides facing, sew the shorter sides together with a ⅜-inch seam allowance. Press or steam seam allowance open.

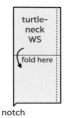

notch

b. Fold the turtleneck in half lengthwise with wrong sides facing and press or steam lightly.

c. Align raw edges with the turtleneck facing the right side of the top. I like to put the seam at the center back. Stitch ⅜ inch from the edge all the way around. Finish raw edges if desired.

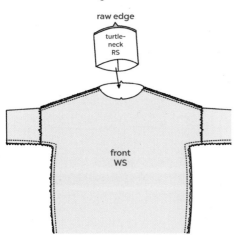

6 Sew sleeve hems. Finish raw edge if desired. Fold hem by ⅜ inch toward the wrong side and press or lightly steam. Edgestitch with a stretch stitch. Repeat for other sleeve.

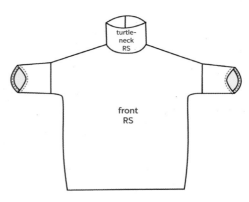

7 Repeat step 6 for the hem. Done!

Variation: Batwing Top

REPLACING THE TURTLENECK WITH A neckband (see T-shirt, page 133), swiftly exaggerating the underarm curve, and removing the sleeves will generate a roomy top that can be laid-back or dressy depending on the fabric you use.

MODIFICATIONS

- In drafting step 2a, lower the front neckline by about 2 inches. This made it more of a crewneck for me.
- In drafting step 2b, extend shoulders a little bit more. I extended mine about 11 inches.
- In drafting step 2f, I reversed the curve under the arms and made it concave, which slimmed down the sides a little. Make sure that your wrist and forearm will fit through the sleeve opening by draping the pattern on your body.
- In drafting step 4, instead of the turtleneck, create a neckband based on neckline measurement (see page 135).
- Follow the construction steps, but skip the turtleneck and sleeve attachment. To attach the neckband, see page 137.

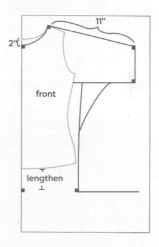

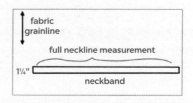

BANDED COLLAR DRESS WITH POCKETS

I LOVE THESE TYPES OF dresses—they feel like pajamas but look a lot more put together and have so many styling options. Wear it with tights, boots, and a chunky knit cowl in the winter, or pair it with cute flats and a silk scarf in the spring. Bonus: it's a surprisingly easy garment to sew up!

SUPPLIES + MATERIALS

Drafting kit (see page 45)

Torso sloper (front and back)

Sleeve sloper

Approx. 3 yards woven fabric

Coordinating thread

ıııııııııııııııııııııııı

FABRIC RECOMMENDATIONS

Cotton lawn, linen, linen blends, chambray, shirting

DRAFTING STEPS

1 Trace the front, back, and sleeve slopers onto separate pieces of paper. Make sure to leave enough space around the traced pieces to make modifications and add seam allowances; here, we will be adding 12 inches or so to the hem, and seam allowances will be ⅜ inch to ¾ inch.

2 Modify front sloper.

a. Draw a horizontal line about 3 inches below the bust apex. If you added a bust dart, you could draw this line below the lower leg of the bust dart, but you would probably want to incorporate the dart into the seam by drawing the horizontal line along the bust apex and using the dart leg positions for the top and bottom pieces. Cut the sloper along this line and tape additional strips of paper that are at least 1 inch high to both upper and lower parts of the sloper (you'll need this to add seam allowance later). Note: subsequent illustrations will not show the taped section.

b. Add ½ inch or so to the side of the front top piece. Horizontally extend the top of the front lower piece by the same amount.

c. Lengthen the lower piece at the hem edge by desired amount (see Sleeveless Dress with Pockets, page 157). I lengthened mine by 14 inches to reach my calves. We will call this the front skirt.

d. Draw a perpendicular, horizontal line from center front to extend the hem sweep by 1 inch to 1½ inches from the lower corner of the sloper.

e. Square corners and curve hems (see page 72).

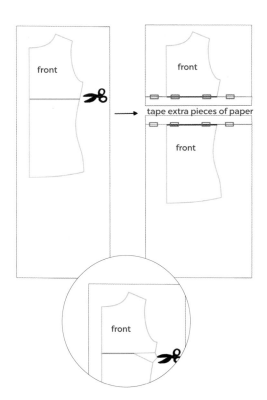

tape extra pieces of paper

front

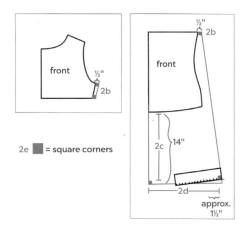

2e ■ = square corners

3 Modify back sloper.

a. Align the back piece with the new, shorter front piece at the bottom of the armhole. Draw a matching line on the back piece and cut apart. Tape strips of paper to the upper and lower parts as you did for the front piece. Subsequent illustrations will not show the taped section.

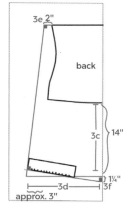

3b ½"

back

3e 2"

back

3c 14"

1¼"

3d 3f

approx. 3"

3g ▪ = square corners

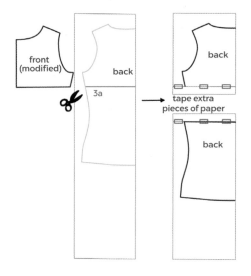

front (modified)

back

3a

back

✂

tape extra pieces of paper

back

b. Add ½ inch to the side of the top piece.

c. Lengthen the lower piece at the hem edge to match the front piece. We will call this the back skirt.

d. Draw a perpendicular, horizontal line from center back to extend the hem sweep by 2 to 3 inches from the lower corner of the sloper.

e. Extend the side horizontally by about 2 inches and connect to hem.

f. Lower the center of the back hem so that it is longer than the front hem by 1¼ inches at the center.

g. Square corners and curve hems (see page 72).

4 Modify the sleeve sloper. Shorten the sleeve so it hits a few inches past your elbow. I determined the measurement by draping the sleeve sloper along my arm and marking where I wanted to shorten it. I shortened mine by 5 inches. Extend each side horizontally by ½ inch. Square corners (see page 72).

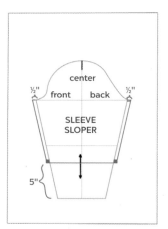

center

½" front back ½"

SLEEVE SLOPER

5"

5 Use the template provided for the pocket. Trace the template and cut it out. ⅜-inch seam allowance is included.

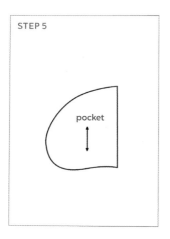

STEP 5

pocket

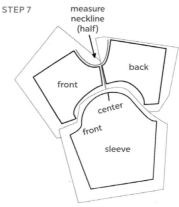

STEP 7

measure
neckline
(half)

front

back

center

front

sleeve

6 Align the pattern pieces and make adjustments as needed (see page 67). Cut out pattern pieces, leaving plenty of room to add seam allowances.

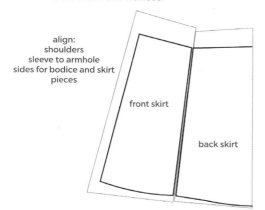

align:
shoulders
sleeve to armhole
sides for bodice and skirt
pieces

front skirt

back skirt

7 Place the pattern pieces with shoulders aligned and measure the neckline (front and back). Keep in mind that this is only half of the neckline, so you'll need to double it. Write down the full neckline measurement (I like to record it on the front pattern piece).

8 Add seam allowance as shown (see page 67). Cut pattern pieces at seam allowance, label, and add grainline (see page 48) and markings. Mark the pocket positions on both front and back pieces (I pin the front pieces together and drape against my body to see where it would feel most comfortable to place the pocket). Also mark the top front piece where you want the front pieces to start overlapping; I marked mine at about 4½ inches from the bottom by using the draping-the-pattern-piece-against-my-body method.

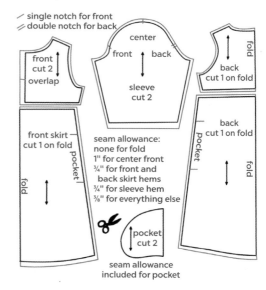

single notch for front
double notch for back

center

front   back

fold

front
cut 2
overlap

sleeve
cut 2

back
cut 1 on fold

front skirt
cut 1 on fold

fold

pocket

seam allowance:
none for fold
1" for center front
¾" for front and
back skirt hems
¾" for sleeve hem
⅜" for everything else

back
cut 1 on fold

pocket

fold

pocket
cut 2

seam allowance
included for pocket

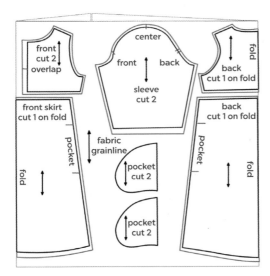

CONSTRUCTION STEPS

1. Place pattern pieces on fabric, trace, and cut out.

2. Draft the neck bias binding directly on the fabric based on the neckline measurement. The binding should be 1¼ inches wide and use the measurement of the full neckline plus 1 inch for the length. Cut out. Optional: I don't usually press folded edges for the bias strips before attaching them, but it allows for more precision, so feel free to do so.

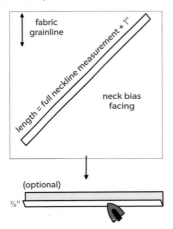

3. Sew center front.

   a. Fold the center edge of the front bodice toward the wrong side by ½ inch twice and press. Repeat for other front piece.

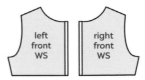

   b. For the left front bodice piece only: edgestitch along both folded edges.

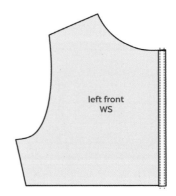

   c. For the right front bodice piece only: edgestitch along the innermost fold all the way down. Then, edgestitch the center fold from the neckline to the mark where the two pieces will begin to overlap.

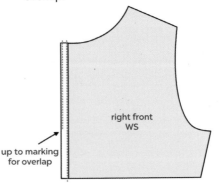

d. Overlap the two pieces by ½ inch with the right piece on top and baste about ¼ inch from the bottom edge. Stitch the overlapped layers together, starting from where you left off in the previous step.

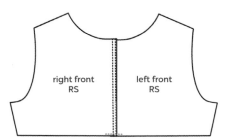

right front
RS

left front
RS

It's easier to do this by sewing with the gathered side facing up. Press seam allowance toward bodice and topstitch. Remove gathering stitches.

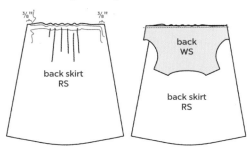

³/₈"

³/₈"

back skirt
RS

back
WS

back skirt
RS

4 Assemble front pieces. Sew front skirt to front bodice with right sides together and a ⅜-inch seam allowance. Finish raw edges and press seam allowance toward bodice. Topstitch.

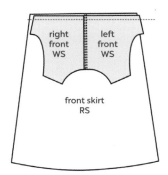

right
front
WS

left
front
WS

front skirt
RS

5 Assemble back pieces. Without back-stitching, leaving ⅜ inch of space on each end and with the longest stitch you have available, sew two parallel lines, ¼ inch and ⅝ inch from top edge. Pull threads to gather the top of the back skirt. With right sides together, sew back skirt and back bodice with ⅜-inch seam allowance, evenly distributing the gathers as you sew.

6 Attach pockets. With right sides together, sew one set of pockets and front piece together at markings with a ⅜-inch seam allowance. Repeat for back piece and other set of pockets. Finish raw edges and press pockets away from dress. Under-stitch (see page 51) seam allowance to the pockets about ⅛ inch from seam.

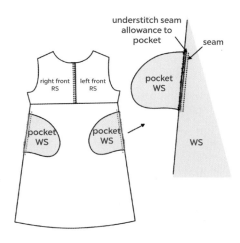

understitch seam allowance to pocket

seam

right front
RS

left front
RS

pocket
WS

pocket
WS

pocket
WS

WS

7 Sew shoulders. With right sides together, align shoulders of front and back pieces and sew with a ⅜-inch seam allowance. Finish raw edges and press seam allowance toward back.

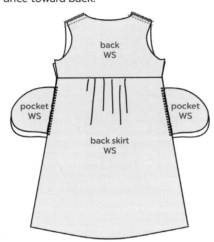

8 Attach sleeves. With right sides together and lining up the markings, attach sleeves with a ⅜-inch seam allowance. Finish raw edges and press seam allowance toward sleeve.

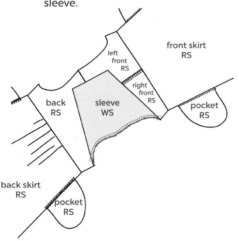

9 Sew sleeves, sides, and pockets. With right sides together, pin and sew the bottom of the sleeve and down the side with a ⅜-inch seam allowance, pivoting at the armpit and at the top corner of the pocket. Sew around the pocket bag, then pivot at the bottom of the pocket and continue sewing down the side to the hem. Repeat for other sleeve and side. Finish raw edges and press.

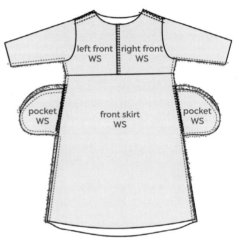

10 Attach neck bias binding.

a. If you haven't already, fold one of the long edges of the bias binding toward the wrong side by ⅜ inch and press. Then, fold the short edges toward the wrong side by ½ inch and press. Optional: press the binding into a curve.

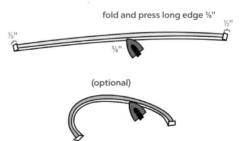

b. With the right side of the binding on the wrong side of the neckline, align the raw edges and stitch, starting at the center back and sewing toward the neck opening, with a ⅜-inch seam allowance. This is to prevent the collar from curling. Sew the second half, then trim seam allowance in half.

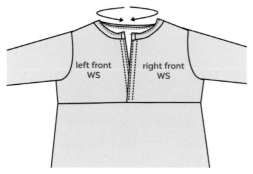

c. Fold the pre-pressed folded edge of the binding toward the right side to enclose the raw edges and topstitch, again, sewing from the center back toward neck opening.

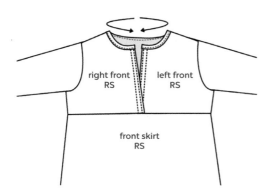

11 Sew sleeve hems. Fold sleeve hem by ⅜ inch toward wrong side and press. Fold another ⅜ inch and press again. Edgestitch along fold. Repeat for other sleeve.

12 Repeat step 11 for hem. All done!

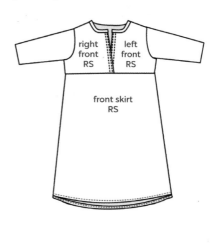

Variation: Button-Down Tunic

TO CREATE A VERSATILE TUNIC top, simplify the silhouette by removing the gathering at the back, extending the front for both the upper and lower pieces to create a button placket, and omitting the lower back hem and pockets.

EXTRA SUPPLIES + MATERIALS

½-inch buttons—as needed (I used 8)

Buttonhole foot

MODIFICATIONS

- In drafting step 2c, lengthen the hem to a tunic length. I lengthened mine 5 inches from the lower corner of the sloper to hit between my thighs and knees, draping the sloper against my body to determine how much I would need to add for the hem. I added only about ½ to the hem width.

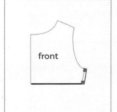

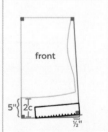

- In drafting step 3:

  a. Skip step 3a.

  b. In step 3c, lengthen to match the front piece.

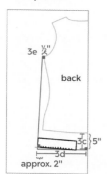

  c. In drafting step 3d, draw a perpendicular, horizontal line from center back to extend the hem sweep by about 2 inches from lower corner of sloper.

  d. In drafting step 3e, extend horizontally under the arm by ½ inch.

  e. Skip drafting step 3f.

- In drafting step 8, add 1½ inches seam allowance for the upper and lower front pieces.

- After construction step 2, instead of overlapping the front pieces, create the button placket. With right sides facing, sew corresponding top and bottom front pieces together with a ⅜-inch seam allowance. Finish raw edges and press seam allowance toward upper piece. Topstitch. Repeat for other top and bottom front pieces.

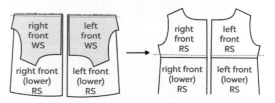

- Fold and press the center edge of one of the front bodice pieces toward the wrong side by ⅝ inch twice. Edgestitch along folded edge. Repeat for other front bodice piece.

- Skip to construction step 7.

- In construction step 9, ignore the pocket instructions.

- To sew buttonholes and buttons, refer to the Button-Down V-Neck Top, page 146, for further instructions, but start the first button about 5 inches from the top.

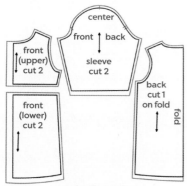

seam allowance:
none for fold
1½" for center front
¾" for front, back,
and sleeve hems
⅜" for everything else

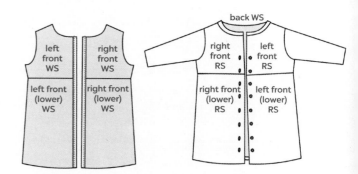

‖‖‖‖‖‖‖‖‖‖‖‖‖‖‖‖‖‖‖‖‖‖‖‖

BOTTOMS

‖‖‖‖‖‖‖‖‖‖‖‖‖‖‖‖‖‖‖‖‖‖‖‖

ELASTIC-WAISTED SHORTS
WITH SLASH POCKETS

WHEN MADE WITH LINEN, THE look is very casual chic, but these also make fantastic pajama shorts (especially if you skip the pockets).

Note: If there are darts in your sloper, keep the darts folded while drafting the modifications; for me, it's helpful to see what my actual waist width is when drafting patterns. When adding to the width of the waist, keep in mind that you want to be able to pull the bottoms up around the fullest part of your body, so a good rule of thumb is to make your waist width equal the fullest part below your waist (typically your full hip).

SUPPLIES + MATERIALS

Drafting kit (see page 45)

Lower body sloper (front and back)

Approx. 1½ yards woven fabric

Approx. ¼ yard woven fabric for pocket lining (if not using the same fabric as shorts)

1¼-inch elastic to fit your preferred waist plus seam allowance

Coordinating thread

Safety pin/bodkin

Optional: lightweight fusible interfacing for pockets

ıııııııııııııııııııııı

FABRIC RECOMMENDATIONS

For shorts: light to mid-weight linen, linen-blends, denim, chambray; for pocket lining (if adding pockets): lighter weight cotton

DRAFTING STEPS

1. Trace the front and back lower body slopers on a piece of paper from waist to mid-thigh (or higher, depending on your preference). Make sure to leave enough room around the traced pieces to make modifications and add seam allowances.

2. Modify front sloper.

   a. Straighten top and extend front waist by about ¾ inch.

   b. Lower the top edge of waistline by 1½ inches. This is because we will be adding a waistband and want the waistband to sit at the preferred waist.

   c. Draw a new curve from extended point from previous step, tapering at the bottom of the curve, as shown.

   d. Extend hem width about ½ inch on each side. Optional: I find that I need to angle and lower the hem at the inseam; otherwise, the shorts tend to ride up in an uncomfortable way. Lower the inseam hem by about ½ inch and curve the hem edge down to meet it.

   e. Connect bottom of crotch curve and side to widened hem.

   f. Square corners (see page 72).

3. Modify back sloper.

   a. Horizontally extend 1 inch at top of the crotch curve, redrawing the curve to taper at the bottom of the curve.

   b. Add about ½ inch to side.

   c. Lower the top edge of waistline by 1½ inches. This is because we will be adding a waistband and want the waistband to sit at the preferred waist.

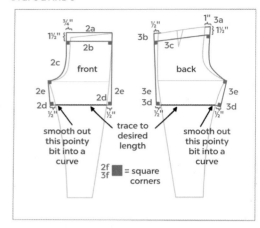

   d. Extend hem width ½ inch on each side. Optional: angle and lower the hem at the inseam by an additional ½ inch as on the front piece.

   e. Connect bottom of crotch curve and side to widened hem.

   f. Square corners (see page 72).

4. Create pockets. You will be creating two pieces: the pocket facing and the pocket lining.

   a. Draw a diagonal line on the front shorts piece for the slash pocket opening, starting about 4 inches horizontally along the waist from the side edge to about 6 inches down the side. Place your hand on the line to make sure your hand will fit.

   b. Make the pocket facing. Place a piece of tracing paper on top of the front piece, and trace the upper right corner, including the diagonal line. Leave plenty of space and draft the pocket facing as shown. You don't need to be too precise here, but a generous curve for the bottom left part of the pocket is what you're aiming for. Just make sure the curved section of the pocket doesn't extend too close to the center (the pocket lining will feel bulky and uncomfortable) or drop past the hem (the pocket lining will end up peeking out from the hem).

c. Make the pocket lining. Trace the pocket facing piece. For this piece you only need up to the diagonal line (but we'll be adding seam allowance, so don't cut anything out yet!).

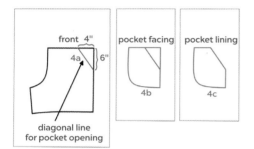

5 Draft waistband. Measure the front and back pieces at the waist and add the measurements together. This is half of the waist measurement. Draw a rectangle with the half-waist length and a height of 3¼ inches.

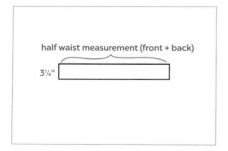

6 Align the pattern pieces and make adjustments as needed (see page 67). Cut out pattern pieces, leaving plenty of room to add seam allowances.

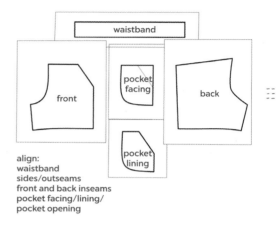

7 Add seam allowance as shown (see page 67). Cut pattern pieces at seam allowance, label, and add grainline (see page 48) and markings.

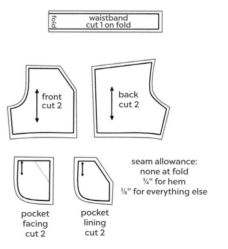

CONSTRUCTION STEPS

1. Place pattern pieces on fabric, trace, and cut out.

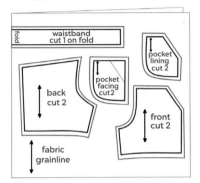

2. Optional: staystitch (see page 51) or iron fusible interfacing to diagonal sections of the pockets and shorts pieces to prevent them from stretching out.

(optional)

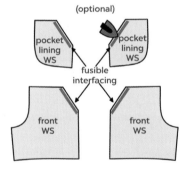

3. Sew pockets.

a. With right sides together, sew pocket lining and corresponding front piece at the pocket opening with a ⅜-inch seam allowance. Trim the lining seam allowance only to about ¼ inch.

b. Flip lining so wrong sides are facing and press.

c. Topstitch along angled edge.

STEP 3

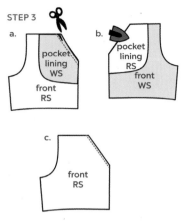

d. Align the wrong side of the front piece on the right side of the facing (sandwiching the pocket lining). Pin the curved edges, then secure the facing to the waist and side of the front piece. Form the pocket bag: sew along the curved edges only with a ⅜-inch seam allowance (do not sew onto the shorts piece). Finish raw edges. Baste side and top edge of pocket to the shorts about ¼ inch from edge.

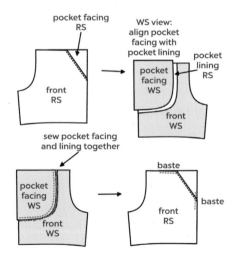

Repeat for other pocket.

4 Sew crotch curves. With right sides together, sew the two front pieces together along the center crotch curve with a ⅜-inch seam allowance. Finish raw edges and press. Repeat for back pieces.

5 Sew inseam. With front and back right sides together, sew the inseam with a ⅜-inch seam allowance. To reduce bulk, alternate the directions of the seam allowance at the inseam. Finish raw edges and press.

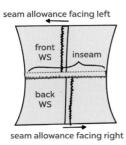

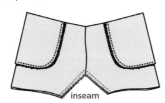

6 Sew sides. With right sides together, sew one side with a ⅜-inch seam allowance. Repeat for other side. Finish raw edges and press toward back.

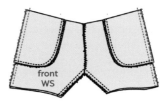

7 Attach waistband to shorts.

a. With right sides together, sew along the short edge of waistband with a ⅜-inch seam allowance. Press seam allowance open.

b. With right sides together and raw edges aligned, sew waistband to shorts with a ⅜-inch seam allowance. I like to place the waistband seam at the center back. Press seam allowance toward waistband.

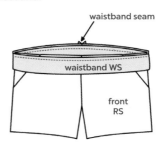

c. Fold the raw edge (the part not sewn to the shorts) toward the waistband by ⅜ inch and press. Wrap the folded edge over to the wrong side of the shorts, just past the seam.

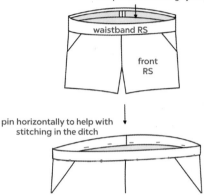

fold toward wrong side by ⅜", press, then press folded edge just past seam

waistband RS

front RS

pin horizontally to help with stitching in the ditch

d. Either hand-sew the waistband (for greater accuracy) or stitch in the ditch (see page 51) from the right side, making sure to leave an opening of about 1½ inches at the back.

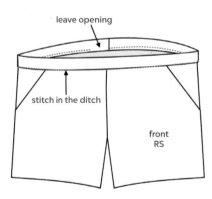

leave opening

stitch in the ditch

front RS

8 Insert elastic. Wrap the elastic around your waist for a snug, but not too tight, fit. Add ¾-inch seam allowance and cut the elastic. Insert elastic through the opening and, using a safety pin or bodkin, thread it through the waistband casing. Be careful not to twist the elastic. Overlap and sew the elastic ends together with a zigzag stitch. Try on the shorts to check the fit and adjust as needed. Slip-stitch opening closed (see page 50).

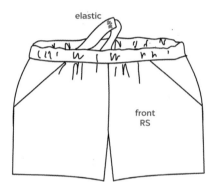

elastic

front RS

9 Sew hem. Fold hem by ⅜ inch toward the wrong side and press. Fold another ⅜ inch and press again. Edgestitch along fold. Press and all done!

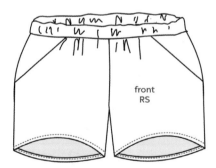

front RS

Variation: Drawstring-Waistband Shorts

I'VE SEWN A LOT OF elastic-waist shorts in my lifetime. This combination of elastic with a drawstring gives more control of the fit. The drawstring also adds a decorative element. To accommodate this modified design, you'll just draft the waistband to be a little taller, sew some extra elastic casings, and add a couple of buttonholes to thread the drawstring.

EXTRA SUPPLIES + MATERIALS

Buttonhole foot

¼-inch elastic to fit your preferred waist plus seam allowance

Lightweight fusible interfacing for buttonholes

Cord or some type of drawstring that is the length of elastic + approx. 12 inches

Optional: awl

MODIFICATIONS

• In drafting step 5, make the waistband height 4 inches. Mark a line to indicate the center front on the waistband and designate which half of the waistband, when folded over, will be outward-facing on the shorts; this will be the lower half of the waistband. Iron a 2-inch by ¾-inch piece of fusible interfacing on the wrong side of the lower half of the waistband. About 1¼ inches from the bottom and ¾ inch from the center front line on each side, poke a hole with an awl. If you do not have an awl, you could mark with chalk or use the tip of small scissors.

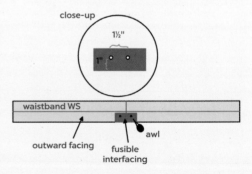

- Using the holes as a guide for the center of each buttonhole, use a marking tool to draw ½-inch lines for the buttonholes. Switch to your buttonhole presser foot and stitch buttonholes. Open them with a seam ripper.

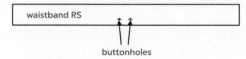

- Proceed up to construction step 7. When sewing the short edge of the waistband, leave an opening of about 2 inches toward the inside-facing top edge.

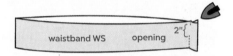

- Attach the waistband to the shorts all the way around (you won't need to leave an opening, since you created one for the waistband in the previous step), making sure that the buttonholes are positioned facing outward at the center front. Follow step 7c and 7d for the waistband.
- Starting at the center back seam opening, sew two parallel lines ½ inch apart for the elastic and drawstring casings.

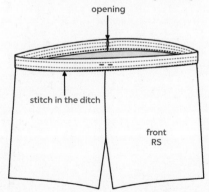

- Thread ¼-inch elastic lengths through the top and bottom casings using a safety pin or small bodkin, and sew ends together.

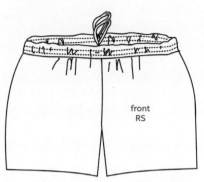

- Thread drawstring through the buttonholes of the middle casing using a safety pin or small bodkin. Check the fit, and slip-stitch opening closed. Knot drawstring ends, then you're done!

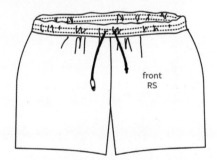

WIDE-LEG PANTS WITH FLAT-FRONT WAISTBAND + ELASTIC BACK

THESE PANTS PROVIDE THE BEST of two worlds: the comfort of an elastic waist and the more polished look of a flat-front waistband. My wide-leg linen pants are a wardrobe staple—I've sewn quite a few! I love the clean lines here, but it's easy-peasy to add inseam pockets (see Sleeveless Dress with Pockets, page 157) or slash pockets (see Elastic-Waisted Shorts with Slash Pockets, page 193).

DRAFTING STEPS

1. Trace the front and back lower body slopers on a piece of paper. Make sure to leave enough room around the traced pieces to make modifications and add seam allowances. These pants are quite wide, so you want at least 15 inches of extra space around each sloper.

SUPPLIES + MATERIALS

Drafting kit (see page 45)

Lower body sloper (front and back)

Approx. 2½ yards woven fabric for pants

Approx. ½ yard interfacing (mid-weight Pellon is good)

¾-inch elastic to fit your preferred waist plus seam allowance

Coordinating thread

Safety pin/bodkin

FABRIC RECOMMENDATIONS

Light to mid-weight linen, denim, bottom weight cotton

If there are darts in your sloper, see note on page 193.

2 Modify front sloper.

a. Shorten pant legs by desired length. My preference for wide-leg pants is about 3 inches above my ankles. Extend the hem line to be wider than the entire sloper width. I made mine a couple of inches past my full hip.

b. Straighten and extend the waist by about ½ inch. Horizontally extend crotch depth by about ½ inch, and redraw curve following the shape of the original curve.

c. Lower the top edge by ¾ inch. This is because we will be adding a waistband and want the waistband to sit at the pre-ferred waist. Connect to 2b.

d. Widen pant legs. Draw a vertical line from the top of the side to desired hem. Draw a vertical line from the top of the inseam/crotch to the hem. My pant leg ended up about 13 inches wide.

e. Square corners (see page 72).

3 Modify back sloper.

a. Shorten pant legs to match front.

b. Extend the waist by about 1 inch on each side.

c. Lower the top edge by ¾ inch. This is because we will be adding a waistband and want the waistband to sit at the preferred waist.

d. Horizontally extend the top of inseam/crotch about ⅛ inch. Redraw curve, following the shape of the original curve.

e. Widen pant legs. Draw a vertical line from the top of the side to desired hem. Draw a vertical line from the top of the

inseam to the hem. Since the width of the back pant piece will be wider than the front, the pant leg width will also be wider than the front pant leg width.

f. Square corners (see page 72).

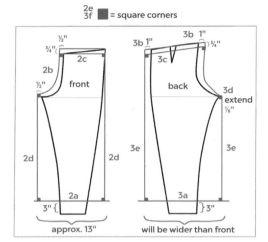

4 Draft waistbands. Match the length of the front waistband to the front pant piece and make the height 2¼ inches. Match the length of the back waistband to the back pant piece and make the height 2¼ inches as well.

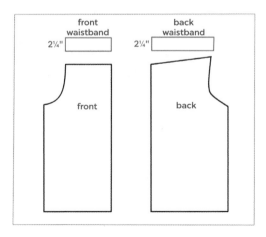

5 Align the pattern pieces and make adjustments as needed (see page 67). Cut out pattern pieces, leaving plenty of room to add seam allowances.

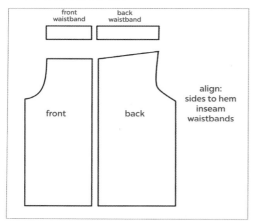

front waistband   back waistband

front   back

align:
sides to hem
inseam
waistbands

6 Add seam allowance as shown (see page 67). Cut pattern pieces at seam allowance, label and add grainline (see page 48) and markings.

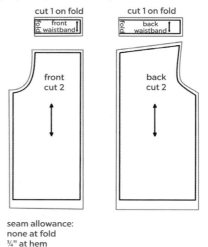

cut 1 on fold   cut 1 on fold

fold front waistband   fold back waistband

front
cut 2   back
cut 2

seam allowance:
none at fold
¾" at hem
⅜" for everything else

CONSTRUCTION STEPS

1 Place pattern pieces on fabric, trace, and cut out.

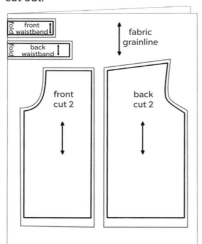

front waistband

back waistband

fabric grainline

front
cut 2   back
cut 2

2 Trace the front waistband pattern piece on fusible interfacing and cut out. (I like to cut inside the line to make the interfacing a little smaller so that there is less bulk.)

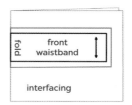

fold   front
waistband

interfacing

3 Sew crotch curves. With right sides together, sew front pant pieces along the center crotch curve with a ⅜-inch seam allowance. Finish raw edges and press. Repeat for back pant pieces.

4 Sew inseam. With front and back right sides together, sew the inseam with a ⅜-inch seam allowance. To reduce bulk where the seams meet, alternate the directions of the crotch seam allowances. Finish raw edges and press.

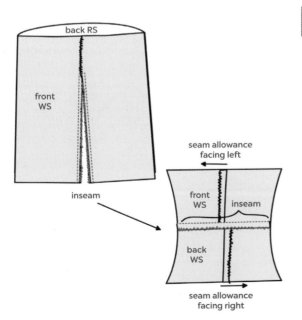

5 Sew sides. With right sides together, sew the side with a ⅜-inch seam allowance. Repeat for other side. Finish raw edges and press seam allowance toward back.

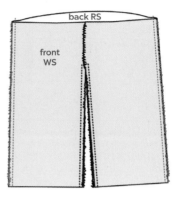

6 Attach waistband.

a. With right sides together, sew front and back waistbands together along the short edges with a ⅜-inch seam allowance, but leave an opening of about ⅜ inch. Repeat on other side. Press seam allowance open.

b. With right sides together and raw edges and side seams aligned, attach waistband to pants with a ⅜-inch seam allowance, making sure that the opening in the waistband seam is positioned as shown. Press seam allowance toward waistband.

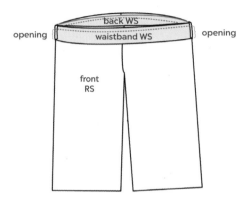

opening — back WS / waistband WS — opening

front RS

c. Fold the raw edge (the part not sewn to the pants) toward the wrong side by ⅜ inch and press.

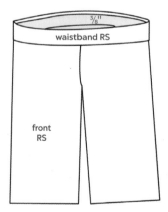

3/8"

waistband RS

front RS

d. Pin the folded edge to the wrong side of the pants just past the seam, and either hand-sew the waistband (for greater accuracy) or stitch in the ditch from the right side (see page 51).

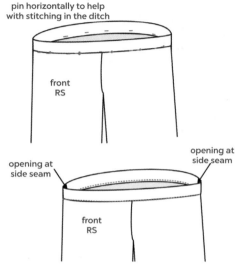

pin horizontally to help with stitching in the ditch

front RS

opening at side seam

opening at side seam

front RS

7 Insert elastic. Wrap the elastic around your waist for a snug, but not too tight, fit and cut in half. Insert elastic through one of the side openings and, using a safety pin or bodkin, thread it through the back waistband casing. When the free end is about 1 inch from the side seam, stitch elastic in place. Pull the other end of the elastic out beyond the other side opening to gather the back waistband. Be careful not to twist the elastic. Safety pin or pin elastic in place and try the pants on for fit. Adjust as needed. Secure the other end of the elastic about 1 inch from the side seam toward the back. Pull the elastic end out of the opening and trim to about ¼ inch. Making sure that the gathering is minimal on the front, smooth out the front waistband and slip-stitch openings

closed. Tip: Attaching safety pins on both ends of the elastic and pinning one end to the opening will anchor it and prevent it from getting lost inside the casing.

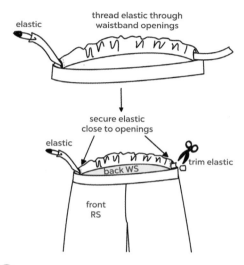

elastic

thread elastic through
waistband openings

secure elastic
close to openings

elastic

back WS

trim elastic

front
RS

8 Sew hem. Fold hem by ⅜ inch toward the wrong side and press. Fold another ⅜ inch and press again. Edgestitch along fold. Press and all done!

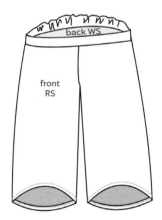

back WS

front
RS

Variation: Straight-Leg Pants with Curved Pockets

THE CURVED POCKETS AND LONGER, slimmer legs make these pants a lovely addition to the wardrobe.

MODIFICATIONS

- In drafting steps 2a and 2d, adjust pant leg hem and width as desired. I kept the hem length the same as the sloper and added about ½ inch on each side of the pant leg hem.

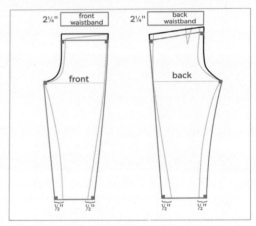

- After drafting step 3, draft the curved pockets. Use the same method as slash pockets (see Elastic-Waisted Shorts with Slash Pockets, page 193), but curve the opening instead using a French curve.

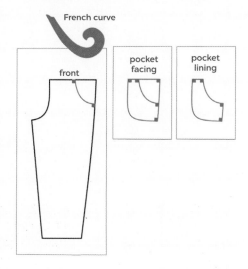

- Here are all the pieces you'll need:

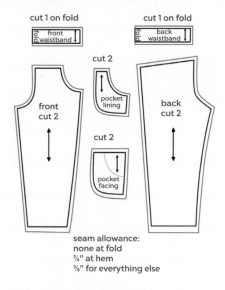

seam allowance:
none at fold
¾" at hem
⅜" for everything else

- Follow the Wide-Leg Pants construction steps, using construction steps 2 and 3 from the Elastic-Waisted Shorts with Slash Pockets pattern, page 193, to sew in the pockets.

SLIM-FIT SIDE ZIP PANTS

I LIKE TO THINK OF these as "Audrey Hepburn Pants"—the evocative cigarette pants of yore. They're eternally stylish and pair well with a woven tee (see left). Use a stretch twill or stretch denim for this pattern to make fitting easier. If you haven't installed an invisible zipper before, I promise it's not as scary as it sounds!

SUPPLIES + MATERIALS

Drafting kit (see page 45)

Lower body sloper (front and back)

Approx. 2¾ yards woven fabric

If using different fabric for the waistband facing: ¼ yard of fabric

7- to 9-inch invisible zipper (longer is okay, since zippers can be shortened)

Coordinating thread

Invisible zipper foot

Optional: regular zipper foot, approx. ½ yard fusible interfacing

ɪɪɪɪɪɪɪɪɪɪɪɪɪɪɪɪɪɪɪɪɪɪɪ

FABRIC RECOMMENDATIONS

Stretch twill, stretch denim

DRAFTING STEPS

1 Trace the front and back lower body slopers on a piece of paper. Make sure to leave enough room around the traced pieces to make modifications and add seam allowances.

2 Make modifications to the traced slopers.

a. Adjust hem as desired. I shortened mine by about ¼ inch

b. Add about ⅛-inch ease to the sides as shown

c. Lower the top edge by ¾ inch. This is because we will be adding a waistband and want the waistband to sit at the preferred waist.

d. In my case, since I'm pretty much flat all around and I knew these would be sewn in a fabric with some stretch, I was able to do away with darts. If you would like more shaping, make sure to transfer darts from your sloper.

e. Square corners (see page 72).

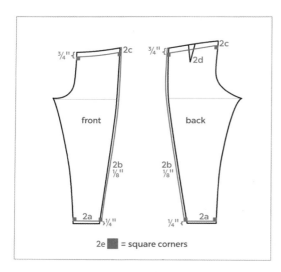

3 Draft the waistband. If applicable, fold dart(s) and temporarily tape down. Place a piece of tracing paper on top and draw a waistband 1½ inches high, following the curve of the waist. Repeat for back piece. Note which side will be on the fold (center back and center front).

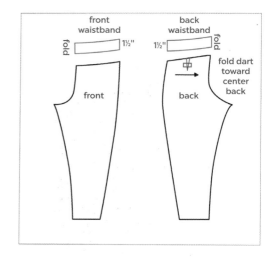

4 Align the pattern pieces and make adjustments as needed (see page 67). Cut out pattern pieces, leaving plenty of room to add seam allowances.

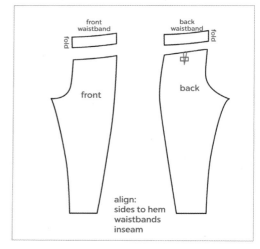

5 Add seam allowance as shown (see page 67). Keep dart(s) folded to add seam allowances. Cut pattern pieces at seam allowance (keep the dart folded!), label and add grainline (see page 48) and markings.

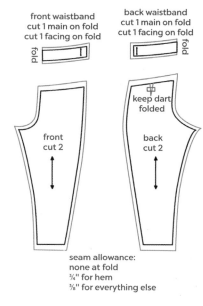

front waistband
cut 1 main on fold
cut 1 facing on fold

back waistband
cut 1 main on fold
cut 1 facing on fold

fold

fold

keep dart folded

front cut 2

back cut 2

seam allowance:
none at fold
¾" for hem
⅜" for everything else

CONSTRUCTION STEPS

1 Place pattern pieces on fabric, trace, and cut out. Make sure to unfold dart(s) to trace onto fabric. If using a different fabric for the waistband facing, trace front and back waistbands on that fabric and cut out. It's helpful to mark or cut notches at the bottom of the front and back waistbands to differentiate them to make assembly easier later.

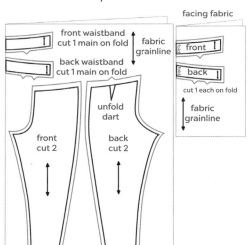

front waistband
cut 1 main on fold

back waistband
cut 1 main on fold

fabric grainline

facing fabric

front

back

cut 1 each on fold

fabric grainline

unfold dart

front cut 2

back cut 2

2 Optional: trace waistband facing on fusible interfacing and cut out. Iron interfacing onto wrong side of facing.

(optional)

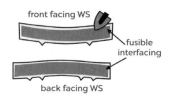

front facing WS

fusible interfacing

back facing WS

3 Sew darts, if applicable (see page 69). Press toward center.

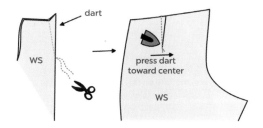

dart

WS

press dart toward center

WS

sewing love

4 Sew crotch curves. With right sides together, sew front pant pieces along the center crotch curve with a ⅜-inch seam allowance. Finish raw edges and press. Repeat for the back pant pieces.

5 Prepare sides: finish raw edges on the sides.

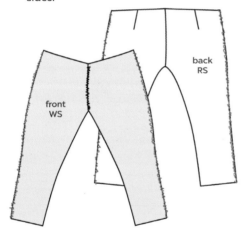

6 Sew inseam. With right sides together, sew the inseam with a ⅜-inch seam allowance. To reduce bulk, sew with crotch seam allowances in alternating directions. Finish raw edges and press.

STEP 6

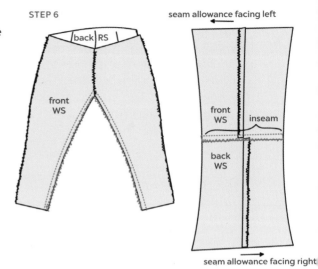

7 Sew outseam. With right sides together, sew only the left outseam as shown (it's actually the right leg) with a ⅜-inch seam allowance. Press seam allowance open. Leave the other side open for now.

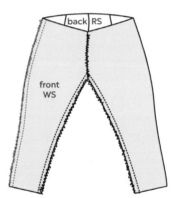

8 Assemble waistband.

a. With right sides together and front waistband on top, sew along the short edge of the waistband on the left side with a ⅜-inch seam allowance. Press seam allowance open. Do not sew other side.

sew left edge for waistband

b. Repeat for waistband facing, but sew on opposite (right) side. Press seam allowance open, then fold the bottom long edge toward the wrong side by ⅜ inch and press.

back facing RS
front facing RS

sew right edge for waistband facings

c. With right sides together, sew waistband and facing with a ⅜-inch seam allowance along top edge (the side opposite the folded waistband facing edge). Trim seam allowance to about ⅛ inch.

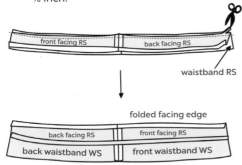

front facing RS   back facing RS

waistband RS

folded facing edge

back facing RS   front facing RS

back waistband WS   front waistband WS

9 Attach waistband to pants. With right sides together and raw edges and side seams aligned, sew waistband to pants with a ⅜-inch seam allowance. Finish raw edges and press seam allowance toward waistband.

STEP 9

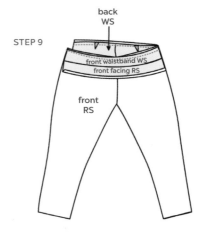

back
WS

front waistband WS
front facing RS

front
RS

10 Insert invisible zipper. Switch to an invisible zipper foot. Then lightly press the coils of the zipper to flatten them out (I don't seem to need to do this with my zipper foot, but it can be helpful).

a. Pin one side of zipper as shown with right side of the zipper facing down and aligned with the raw edge of the pants. Make sure that the metal tip of the zipper is positioned about ¼ inch down from where the waistband meets the facing. Fold the top of the zipper under. Pin, clip, or hand-baste the zipper. Stitch along the zipper teeth using the invisible zipper foot.

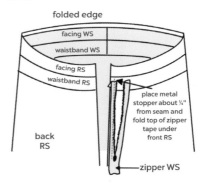

folded edge

facing WS

waistband WS

facing RS
waistband RS

back
RS

place metal stopper about ¼" from seam and fold top of zipper tape under
front RS

zipper WS

b. Close the zipper and, using chalk, mark where the waistband meets the top of the pants on both sides of the zipper. Open the zipper again.

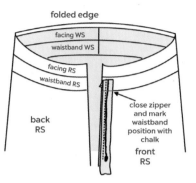

folded edge

facing WS

waistband WS

facing RS

waistband RS

back RS

close zipper and mark waistband position with chalk

front RS

c. Then with right sides facing, pin, clip, or hand-baste the other side of the zipper to the other pant piece, aligning the chalk mark at the designated waistband position. Stitch. Check that the zipper closes properly.

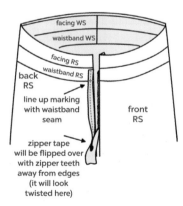

facing WS

waistband WS

facing RS

waistband RS

back RS

line up marking with waistband seam

front RS

zipper tape will be flipped over with zipper teeth away from edges (it will look twisted here)

11 Finish waistband.

a. Switch back to your standard presser foot. With right sides together and the pressed edge of the facing folded down over the zipper, sew waistband edges with a ⅜-inch seam allowance. Trim seam allowance and clip corners.

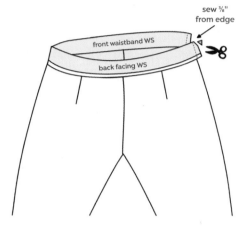

sew ⅜" from edge

front waistband WS

back facing WS

b. Turn right side out, then position the folded edge of the waistband so that it slightly overlaps the seam. Confirm that the zipper still closes smoothly. Hand-sew or stitch in the ditch (see page 51) to secure waistband. Topstitch along upper edge of waistband if desired.

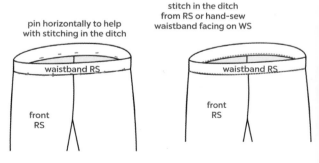

pin horizontally to help with stitching in the ditch

waistband RS

front RS

stitch in the ditch from RS or hand-sew waistband facing on WS

waistband RS

front RS

c. Slip-stitch folded edges of waistband to the zipper tape.

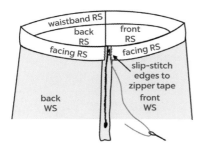

12 Sew outseam with zipper. With right sides together and starting at the bottom of the zipper, stitch all the way down the outseam to the hem with a ⅜-inch seam allowance. Depending on your presser foot, you may end up with a tiny gap at the bottom of your zipper. A regular zipper foot will help with getting closer, but a standard presser foot works pretty well too. Press seam allowance open. Slip-stitch any gap you might have at the bottom of the zipper.

13 Sew hem. Fold hem by ⅜ inch toward the wrong side and press. Fold another ⅜ inch and press again. Edgestitch along fold. Press and all done!

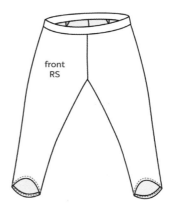

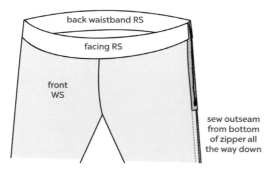

Variation: Leggings

THIS PANTS PATTERN CAN BE easily converted to a leggings pattern, and to do so, I'll show you a different and equally easy way of sewing pant legs.

EXTRA SUPPLIES + MATERIALS

⅜-inch elastic to fit your preferred waist plus seam allowance

Approx. 2 yards stretchy fabric

Ballpoint machine needle

Safety pin or bodkin

FABRIC RECOMMENDATIONS

Performance knit, 4-way stretch knit jersey (See note on page 133 for knit-specific tips.)

MODIFICATIONS

Since the steps are quite different from the Slim-Fit Pants, I will not reference the steps from the project for this variation.

DRAFTING STEPS

1 Make modifications to slopers after tracing front and back lower slopers onto paper.

a. Fold down any darts you may have on your front and back lower slopers.

b. Lower waist by about 1 inch.

c. Since you'll be sewing with knit fabric and you probably don't want baggy leggings, you'll draft with negative ease, which means reducing the seam-line by ¼ inch as shown.

d. Reduce hem width by about 1 inch on each side for a snug fit around the ankles.

e. Align pattern pieces (see page 67) and square corners (see page 72).

f. Draft waistband based on your front plus back waist measurements on the sloper and preferred width. I made mine 2¼ inches wide. This is half of your waist, so we will cut the waistband on the fold.

2 Add seam allowance as shown (see page 67).

DRAFTING STEP 1

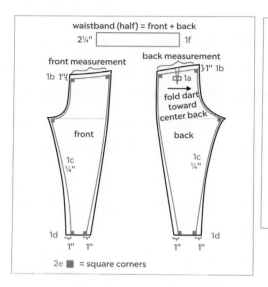

DRAFTING STEP 2

seam allowance:
none at fold
⅜" for
everything else

CONSTRUCTION STEPS

1 Place pattern pieces on fabric, trace, and cut out.

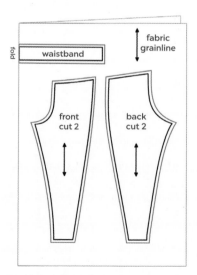

2 Sew pant legs. With right sides together, sew one front leg and one back leg along the side and inseam with a ⅜-inch seam allowance. Repeat for other front and back leg pieces. Finish raw edges if desired.

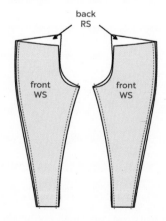

3 Sew crotch curve. Turn one leg right side out and then, with right sides together (as shown: one leg slipped inside the other), sew along crotch curve with a ⅜-inch seam allowance. Finish raw edges if desired.

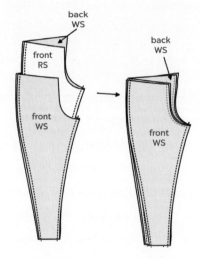

b. Attach waistband. Make sure that the ½-inch elastic opening will end up on the wrong side of the waistband (inside, so the seam will be hidden when wearing). I like to place the seam at the center back. Align raw edges and sew with a ⅜-inch seam allowance all the way around. Finish raw edges if desired.

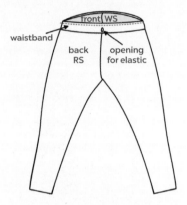

4 Attach waistband.

a. With right sides together, sew short ends of waistband with a ⅜-inch seam allowance, leaving an opening of about ½ inch in the lower half for threading the elastic. Press seam allowance open, and fold in half with wrong sides facing.

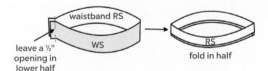

5 Insert elastic. Thread elastic through casing with a safety pin or small bodkin, sew elastic ends together, and slip-stitch (see page 50) opening closed.

6 Sew hem. Finish raw edge of hem if desired. Fold the hem by ⅜ inch and edgestitch (see page 48) with a stretch stitch. All done!

BACK ZIP A-LINE SKIRT

I HAVE OFTEN HEARD THAT A-line skirts are universally flattering. Truth be told, I'm not much of a skirt-wearer, but it seems remiss not to include such a simple, useful skirt.

SUPPLIES + MATERIALS

Drafting kit (see page 45)

Lower Body Sloper (front and back)

Approx. 2¾ yards woven fabric

Approx. ¼ yard contrast fabric, if using different fabric for the waistband facing

7-inch invisible zipper

Coordinating thread

Invisible zipper foot

Optional: regular zipper foot, approx. ½ yard fusible interfacing

ıııııııııııııııııııııııııı

FABRIC RECOMMENDATIONS

Light- to medium-weight linen, denim, bottom weight cotton

DRAFTING STEPS

1 Trace the front and back lower body slopers on a piece of paper. Make sure to leave enough room around the traced pieces to make modifications and add seam allowances.

2 Modify front sloper (if applicable, fold dart as if you are going to sew it, and temporarily tape it toward center front).

a. Draw a straight vertical line for the center fold of skirt front.

b. Lower the top edge by ¾ inch. This is because we will be adding a waistband and want the waistband to hit at the preferred waist.

c. Determine skirt length. I wanted mine to be a midi-skirt so, using my sloper, I marked a spot just past my knee.

d. Determine skirt sweep (a.k.a. hem width) and draw a horizontal line for the hem. I extended my hem 14 inches from the center fold.

e. Connect waist to hem, gently curving the side.

f. Square corners and curve hems (see page 72).

3 Modify back sloper

a. Draw a straight vertical line for the center line of skirt back (note that back will not be on fold).

b. Lower the top edge by ¾ inch. This is because we will be adding a waistband and want the waistband to hit at the preferred waist.

c. Place the front skirt pattern piece on the traced lower back sloper with the outer edge of the waist aligned, then trace the front piece for the side and hem. You may need to extend the hem width to meet the center back vertical line; back pieces tend to be wider than the front to accommodate hips.

d. Square corners and curve hems (see page 72).

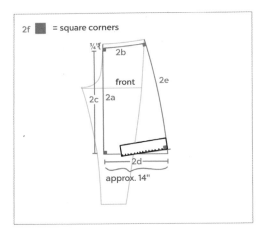

2f ■ = square corners

¾" 2b

front   2e

2c 2a

2d

approx. 14"

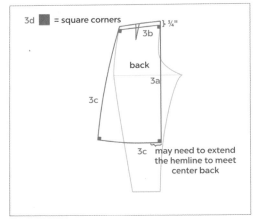

3d ■ = square corners   } ¾"

3b

back

3a

3c

3c may need to extend the hemline to meet center back

4 Draft the waistband. If applicable, fold dart(s) and temporarily tape them down. Place a piece of tracing paper on top and draw a 1¼ inches-high waistband, following the curve of the waist. Repeat for back piece. Tape back waistband piece to the front waistband piece.

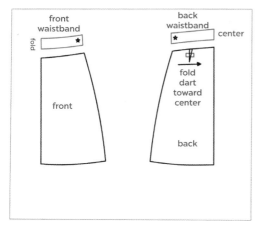

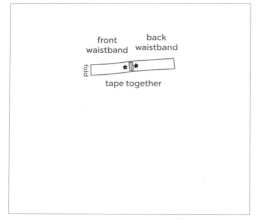

5 Align the pattern pieces and make adjustments as needed (see page 67). Cut out pattern pieces, leaving plenty of room to add seam allowances.

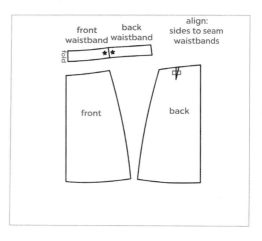

6 Add seam allowance as shown (see page 67). Keep dart(s) folded to add seam allowances. Cut pattern pieces at seam allowance (keep the dart folded!), label, and add grainline (see page 48) and markings. To make assembly easier, mark the top and bottom of the waistband/waistband facing.

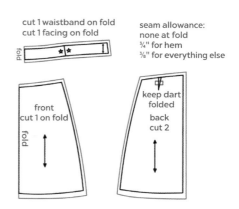

CONSTRUCTION STEPS

1 Place pattern pieces on fabric, trace, and cut out. Unfold dart(s) when tracing.

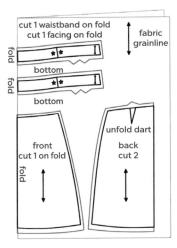

2 Optional: trace waistband facing on fusible interfacing and cut out. Iron interfacing onto wrong side of facing.

(optional)

facing WS   fusible interfacing

3 Sew darts, if applicable (see page 69). Press toward center.

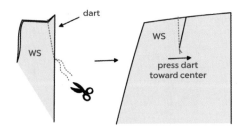

dart

WS

WS

press dart toward center

4 Prepare pieces: finish center back raw edges.

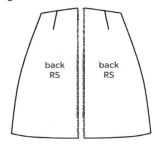

back RS   back RS

5 Sew sides. With right sides together, sew side with a ⅜-inch seam allowance. Repeat for other side. Finish seam allowances and press toward back.

front WS

6 Attach waistband.

a. Fold the bottom long edge of the waistband facing toward wrong side by ⅜ inch and press. With right sides together, sew waistband and facing with a ⅜-inch seam allowance along top edge (the side opposite the folded edge of the waistband facing). Trim the facing seam allowance only to about ⅛ inch. Press seam allowance toward waistband.

facing RS

waistband WS

trim facing seam allowance

b. With right sides together and raw edges aligned, sew waistband to skirt with a ⅜-inch seam allowance.

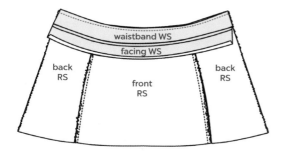

waistband WS
facing WS
back RS
back RS
front RS

7 Insert invisible zipper. Switch to an invisible zipper foot. Then lightly press the coils of the zipper to flatten them out (I don't seem to need to do this with my zipper foot, but it can be helpful).

a. Pin one side of zipper as shown with right side of the zipper facing down and aligned with the raw edge of the skirt. Make sure that the metal tip of the zipper is positioned about ¼ inch down from the seam where the waistband meets the facing. Fold the top of the zipper under. Pin, clip, or hand-baste the zipper. Stitch along the zipper teeth using the invisible zipper foot.

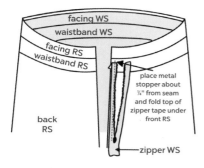

facing WS
waistband WS
facing RS
waistband RS
back RS
place metal stopper about ¼" from seam and fold top of zipper tape under front RS
zipper WS

b. Close the zipper and using chalk, mark where the waistband meets the top of the skirt on both sides of the zipper.

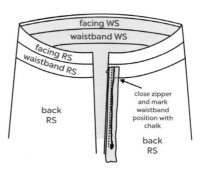

facing WS
waistband WS
facing RS
waistband RS
back RS
close zipper and mark waistband position with chalk
back RS

c. Open the zipper again. Then with right sides facing, pin, clip, or hand-baste the other side of the zipper to the other skirt piece, aligning the chalk mark at the designated waistband position. Stitch. Check that the zipper closes properly.

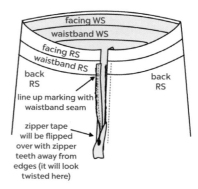

facing WS
waistband WS
facing RS
waistband RS
back RS
back RS
line up marking with waistband seam
zipper tape will be flipped over with zipper teeth away from edges (it will look twisted here)

8 Finish center back. With right sides together and starting at the bottom of the zipper, stitch all the way down the to the hem with a ⅜-inch seam allowance. Depending on your presser foot, you may end up with a tiny gap at the bottom of your zipper. A regular zipper foot will help with getting closer, but a standard presser foot works fine too. Press seam allowance open. Slip-stitch any gap you might have at the bottom of the zipper and at waistband edges along zipper.

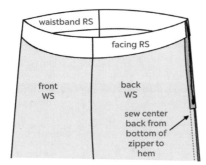

waistband RS
facing RS
front WS
back WS
sew center back from bottom of zipper to hem

9 Finish waistband.

a. Switch back to your standard presser foot. With right sides together and the pressed edge of the facing folded over the zipper, sew waistband edges along center back with a ⅜-inch seam allowance. Trim seam allowance and clip corners.

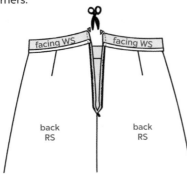

facing WS   facing WS
back RS   back RS

b. Turn right side out, then position the folded edge of the waistband so that it slightly overlaps the seam. Confirm that the zipper still closes smoothly. Hand-sew or stitch in the ditch (see page 51) to secure waistband. Topstitch along upper edge of waistband if desired. Slip-stitch folded edge of waistband to zipper (see page 219).

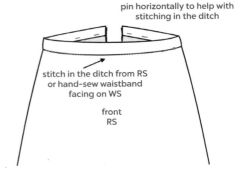

pin horizontally to help with stitching in the ditch

stitch in the ditch from RS or hand-sew waistband facing on WS

front RS

10 Sew hem. Fold hem by ⅜ inch toward the wrong side and press. Fold another ⅜ inch and press again. Edgestitch along fold. Press and all done!

front RS

back WS

Variation: Skirt with Inverted Box Pleat

FOR A CLASSY AND SLIGHTLY retro vibe, try an inverted box pleat! You can make your inverted pleat any size; I made this one 2 inches.

- In construction step 4, start by creating the inverted pleat.

a. With right sides together, fold the skirt front in half and sew 2 inches from the folded edge. Sew about 5 inches down.

b. Open up the front skirt, flatten the fold, and press to create sharp creases along the front. Baste the top of the inverted pleat to secure.

- Follow the rest of the construction steps. To hem the skirt, follow construction step 11, then press the folds into a pleat again.

MODIFICATIONS

- In drafting step 2, add 2 inches to the center front and cut on the fold.

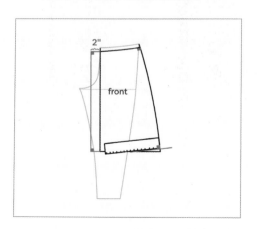

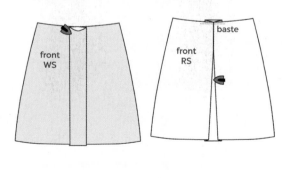

OUTERWEAR

CARDIGAN

THIS RELAXED CARDI MADE OUT of stretchy goodness will keep you so toasty and comfortable, you may find yourself reaching for it on the daily.

SUPPLIES + MATERIALS

Drafting kit (see page 45)

Torso sloper (front and back)

Sleeve sloper

Approx. 2 yards stretchy fabric

Ballpoint machine needle

Coordinating thread

Optional: stay tape

FABRIC RECOMMENDATIONS

Bamboo knit, jersey, tencel, linen jersey (See note on page 133 for knit-specific tips.)

DRAFTING STEPS

1. Trace the torso and sleeve slopers onto a separate piece of paper. If you added a bust dart for your sloper, fold and tape down before tracing, since you won't need darts for knits. Make sure to leave enough room around the traced pieces to make modifications and add seam allowances.

2 Modify front sloper.

a. Shift neck/shoulder point by ½ inch toward outer shoulder.

b. Draw a diagonal line from the new neck/shoulder point to about the middle of the center front.

c. Extend outer shoulder by about ½ inch.

d. Lower bottom of armhole by about ½ inch.

e. Horizontally extend bottom of armhole by about ½ inch.

f. Lengthen hem to desired length. I added 4 inches for the hem.

g. Extend hem width by about 1 inch beyond the lower corner of the sloper, and connect to extended bottom of armhole.

h. Square corners and curve hems (see page 72).

3 Modify back sloper.

a. Raise neckline by ½ inch.

b. Repeat steps c–h from front sloper modifications or trace front sloper.

4 Modify sleeve sloper.

a. Draw a horizontal line about 3 inches below top of sleep cap. Cut along line. Tape a piece of paper underneath the sleeve cap portion. Position the lower part of the sleeve ½ inch from the bottom of the sleeve cap and tape in place. Draw new lines to smooth out the curves.

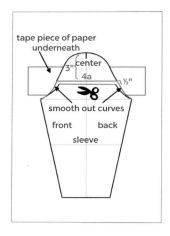

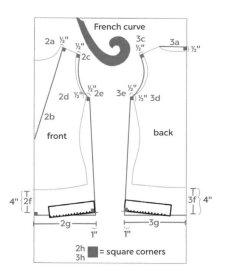

b. Horizontally extend the sides by ¼ inch at bottom of armhole and connect to hem.

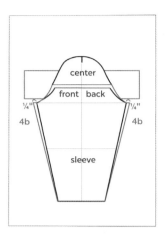

5 Align the pattern pieces and make adjustments as needed (see page 67). Cut out pattern pieces, leaving plenty of room to add seam allowances.

6 Place the pattern pieces with shoulders aligned, and measure the neckline from back to front and continuing all the way down to the hem. Record this number (I like to write it on the front pattern piece). Keep in mind that this is half of the neckline measurement, which is what you will need for drafting the neckband later.

align:
shoulders
sleeve and armhole
sides to hem

measure:
neckline/front
opening (half)

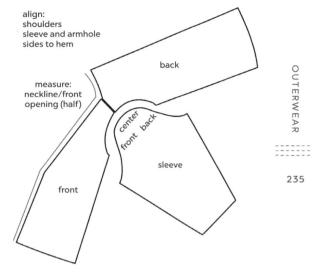

7 Add seam allowance as shown (see page 67). Cut pattern pieces at seam allowance, label, and add grainline (see page 48) and markings.

seam allowance:
¼" for neckline/front opening
¾" for hem
⅜" for everything else

/ = single notch for front
// = double notch for back

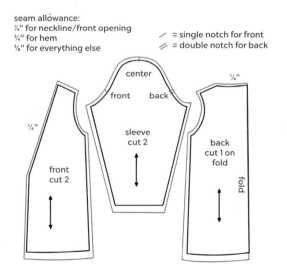

CONSTRUCTION STEPS

1 Place pattern pieces on fabric, trace, and cut out.

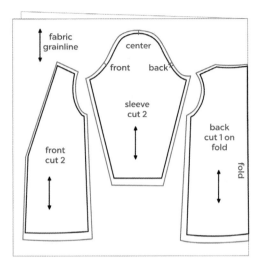

2 Draft the neckband directly on fabric based on neckline measurement plus ¼ inch. I drafted a width of 2 inches. Normally a neckband for a stretch garment would be cut cross grain (see grainline on page 48), which is usually stretchier, but in this case we don't want the neckband to stretch too much, which is why it is drafted on the grainline.

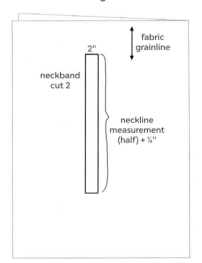

3 Optional: iron stay tape to shoulders and hem.

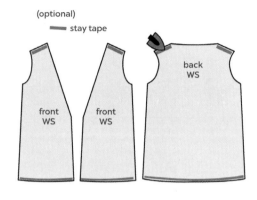

4 Sew shoulders. With right sides together, align shoulders of front and back pieces and sew with a ⅜-inch seam allowance. Finish raw edges if desired.

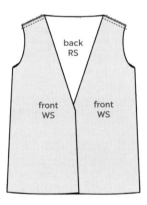

5 Attach sleeves. With right sides together, attach sleeves with a ⅜-inch seam allowance. Finish raw edges if desired.

sewing love

STEP 5

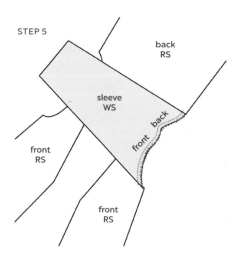

back
RS

sleeve
WS

front
back

front
RS

front
RS

front
RS

6 Sew sleeves and sides. With right sides together, sew the bottom of the sleeve, pivot at the armpit, then continue all the way down the side with a ⅜-inch seam allowance. Repeat for other side. Finish raw edges if desired.

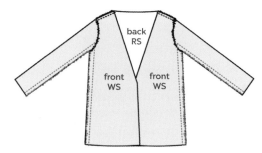

back
RS

front
WS

front
WS

7 Sew sleeve hems. Finish raw edge if desired. Fold edge by ⅜ inch toward the wrong side and press or lightly steam. Edgestitch. Repeat for other sleeve hem.

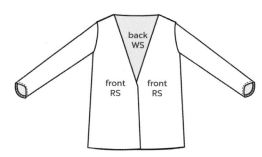

back
WS

front
RS

front
RS

8 Sew hem. Finish raw edge first, if desired. Fold and press hem up by ¾ inch and edgestitch.

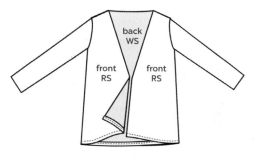

back
WS

front
RS

front
RS

9 Attach neckband.

a. With right sides facing, sew the two neckband pieces together along the short ends on one side with a ¼-inch seam allowance. Finger-press seam allowance open.

b. With right sides facing, fold the bottom edges in half and sew with a ¼-inch seam allowance. Turn right side out and press the entire length of the neckband in half with wrong sides together.

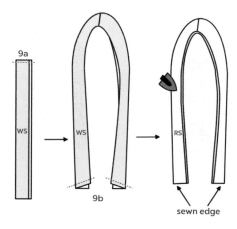

9a

WS

WS

RS

9b

sewn edge

c. Pin the neckband to the right side of the cardigan starting at center back, with raw edges aligned all the way down. I like to fold the back piece in half to form a crease, to which I align the neckband center seam. The bottom of neckband should be flush with the hem. Sew ¼ inch from the edge all the way around. Finish raw edges if desired.

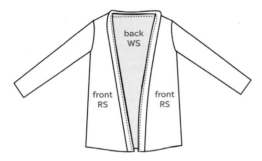

d. Press seam allowance away from neckband and topstitch ⅛ inch from seam to secure seam allowance. I used a long straight stitch (4 millimeters). A stretch stitch or narrow zigzag stitch works too. Then you're finished!

Variation: Cardigan with Curved Hem

CURVING THE LOWER PORTION OF the front piece adds a playful detail. You'll need a longer band to attach all the way around, including the neck, front opening, and entire bottom hem, but otherwise, the steps are nearly identical.

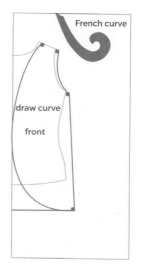

French curve

draw curve

front

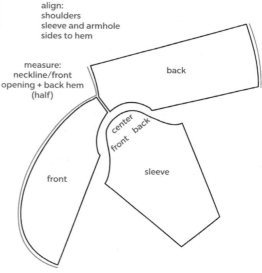

align:
shoulders
sleeve and armhole
sides to hem

measure:
neckline/front
opening + back hem
(half)

back

center
front back

front

sleeve

MODIFICATIONS

- Skip drafting step 2b. After determining hem length, draw a roughly C-shaped curve from the neck/shoulder point to the outer edge of the front hem.
- In drafting step 6, include the back hem measurement.
- In drafting step 7, add only ⅜-inch seam allowance to hem.
- Skip construction step 8.
- In construction step 9, double-check that the neckband length fits all the way around before sewing. Sew both short ends and proceed with the rest of the instructions.

DRAPEY JACKET WITH POCKETS

THE SELLING POINT OF THIS jacket is the cascading front opening, reminiscent of a waterfall. The added fabric provides extra warmth, making this a cozy option for chilly days.

SUPPLIES + MATERIALS

Drafting kit (see page 45)

Torso sloper (front and back)

Approx. 3 to 4 yards fabric

Coordinating thread

⁙⁙⁙⁙⁙⁙⁙⁙⁙⁙⁙⁙⁙⁙⁙⁙⁙⁙⁙⁙⁙⁙⁙⁙⁙

FABRIC RECOMMENDATIONS

Look for extra-wide fabric (at least 60 inches in width if possible) in wool, linen, or medium-weight knit fabric. My fabric was 68 inches wide. (See note on page 133 for knit-specific tips.)

DRAFTING STEPS

1. Trace the torso slopers onto a separate piece of paper. If you added a bust dart for your sloper, fold and tape down before tracing, since there will be plenty of ease added. Make sure to leave enough room around the traced pieces to make modifications and add seam allowances; the front sloper will be extended significantly—by at least 15 inches.

2. Modify front sloper.

   a. Extend shoulder by 6 inches, following the slope of the shoulder.

   b. About 3 inches below the bottom of the armhole, draw a horizontal line that is about 2 inches shorter than the extended shoulder length. Connect the endpoint of the extended shoulder and underarm horizontal line. Drape against your body to make sure your arm will fit.

c. Lengthen hem by about 3 inches.

d. Extend hem width to about the middle of the line from 2b. Draw a line perpendicular to the hem up to connect with that line.

e. Curve underarm.

f. Square corners (see page 72).

g. About ⅜ inch down from the neck/shoulder point, draw a horizontal line perpendicular to the center front line with a length of about 15 inches. Connect the end of this line to the bottom of the center front with a diagonal line.

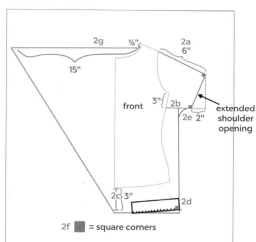

③ Modify back sloper.

a. Repeat steps a–f from the front sloper modifications or trace the front piece.

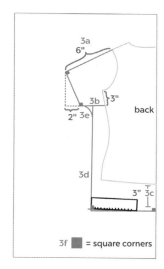

④ Draft sleeve.

a. Measure the extended shoulder opening of the front piece, which is your new armhole. Draw a vertical line on a folded piece of paper with that measurement.

b. Bend your arm slightly and measure the distance between your shoulder and your wrist bone. I find it helpful to secure the end of the measuring tape with washi or clear tape to my wrist, then ease the tape up to measure. Subtract the amount you added to the shoulder width in step 2a, which was 6 inches in my case. This will be your sleeve length. Mark this distance from 4a along the fold.

c. Measure your wrist circumference (if you don't already have this recorded), divide the number in half, and add about 2 inches for the sleeve hem. Draw a vertical line from the 4b marking with this measurement.

d. Connect the endpoints of the vertical lines.

e. Square corners (see page 72).

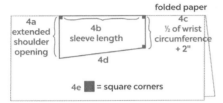

folded paper

| 4a extended shoulder opening | 4b sleeve length | 4c ½ of wrist circumference + 2" |

4d

4e ■ = square corners

Note that the sleeve pattern is drafted on the fold, so add the seam allowance to the half sleeve, then cut and unfold so you have the full sleeve pattern piece.

5. Use the template provided for the pocket. Trace the template and cut it out. A ⅜-inch seam allowance is included.

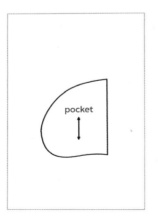

pocket

6. Align the pattern pieces and make adjustments as needed (see page 67). Cut out pattern pieces, leaving plenty of room to add seam allowances.

7. Place the pattern pieces with shoulders aligned and measure the neckline from back to front, all the way across the extended edge. Keep in mind that this is only half of the neckline, so you'll need to double it to draft the neck bias tape later. Write down the full neckline measurement (I like to write it on the front pattern piece).

align:
shoulders
extended shoulder openings and sleeve sides to hem

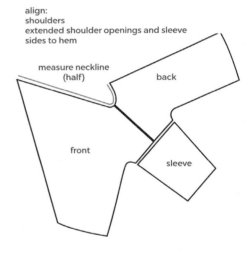

measure neckline (half)

back

front

sleeve

8. Add seam allowances as shown (see page 67). Cut pattern pieces at seam allowance, label, and add grainline (see page 48) and markings. Make sure to mark pocket positions on both front and back pieces by draping the pattern pieces on your body and finding a comfortable position for the pockets.

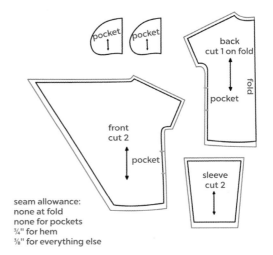

seam allowance:
none at fold
none for pockets
¾" for hem
⅝" for everything else

CONSTRUCTION STEPS

1. Place pattern pieces on fabric, trace, and cut out.

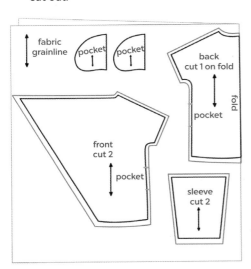

2. Draft bias facing based on neckline measurement. Make the width 1¼ inches and add ½ inch to the neckline measurement for the length. Cut 2.

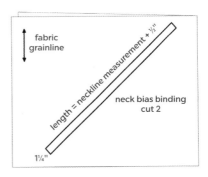

3 Attach pockets.

a. With right sides together, sew one pocket and front piece together at markings with a ⅜-inch seam allowance. Repeat for other front piece and pocket piece. Repeat for back piece and other set of pockets as well.

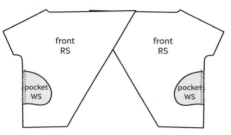

b. If using a fabric that frays, finish raw edges along the pockets. Press pockets away from jacket.

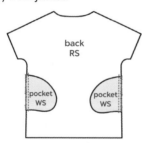

c. Understitch (see page 51) seam allowance to the pockets about ⅛ inch from seam.

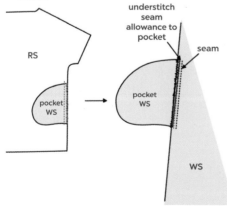

4 Sew shoulders. With right sides together, align shoulders of front and back pieces and sew with a ⅜-inch seam allowance. Finish raw edges for fabrics that fray. Press seam allowance toward back.

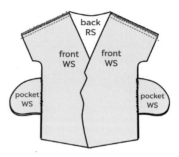

5 Attach sleeves. With right sides together, attach sleeves with a ⅜-inch seam allowance. Finish raw edges if applicable. Press seam allowance toward sleeve.

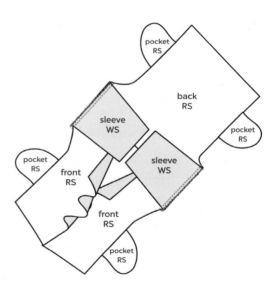

6 Sew sleeves and sides. With right sides together, pin and sew the bottom of the sleeve and down the side with a ⅜-inch seam allowance, pivoting at the armpit and at the top corner of the pocket. Sew around the pocket bag, then pivot at the bottom of the pocket and continue sewing down the side to the hem. Repeat for other sleeve and side. Finish raw edges if applicable and press.

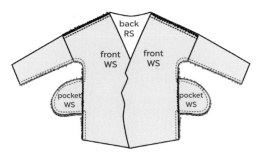

7 Sew front edges. Fold and press the front edge toward the wrong side by ⅜ inch twice, then edgestitch. Press.

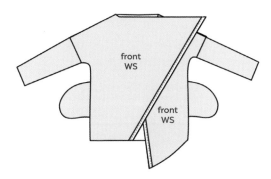

8 Attach neck bias facing.

a. With right sides facing, sew strips of bias tape together with ¼-inch seam allowance at one of the short ends. Fold one of the long edges toward the wrong side by ⅜ inch and press. Fold the short outer edges toward the wrong side by ¼ inch and press.

STEP 8a

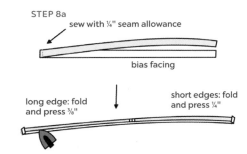

b. With right sides of the jacket and bias facing together and starting at one end, stitch ⅜ inch from the edge all the way to the other end. Trim the seam allowances to about ⅛ inch. Press the seam allowance away from neckline, toward facing.

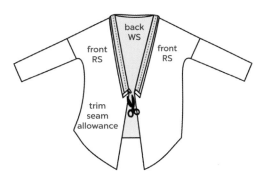

c. Fold and press the facing along the seam toward the wrong side of the top edge, encasing the raw edges. Edgestitch along fold.

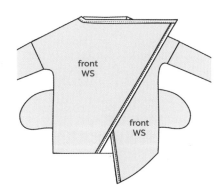

9 Sew sleeve hems. Press sleeve edge toward wrong side by ⅜ inch, press. Fold another ⅜ inch and press. Edgestitch along fold. Repeat for other sleeve. If using a knit fabric, see page 179 to finish sleeve.

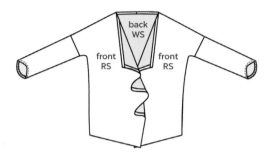

10 Repeat step 9 for the hem. Give it a sturdy press (or lightly steam for knits), and all done!

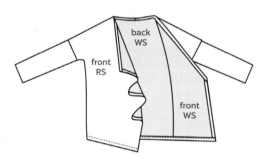

Variation: Minimalist Drapey Jacket

JUST BY REDUCING THE EXTENDED collar length a few inches, you will transform your jacket from frilly and flared to minimal and modern. The shorter collar can be left open or overlapped. Consider lengthening the hem (see page 132), which will create an unlined, retro-style coat with an overlapped collar that's perfect for spring.

MODIFICATIONS

- In drafting step 2c, lengthen the hem. I lengthened the hem by 10 inches.
- In drafting step 2g, extend the front past the center by about 3 inches.
- In drafting step 7, measure the new neckline and adjust the neck bias tape length accordingly in construction step 2.

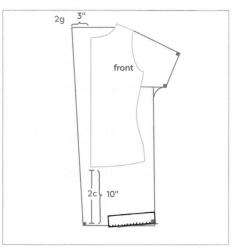

HANTEN COAT

HANTEN IS A JAPANESE STYLE of short coat that's often padded or quilted, though for this version I kept it simple with an easy bagged lining. It's a fuss-free coat with interestingly angled pockets and no closures.

SUPPLIES + MATERIALS

Drafting kit (see page 45)

Torso sloper (front and back)

Approx. 3–4 yards woven fabric for coat

Approx. 3–4 yards woven fabric for lining

Coordinating thread

Optional: fusible interfacing for pockets

FABRIC RECOMMENDATIONS

For coat: denim, mid-weight linen, canvas; for lining: lightweight cotton or brushed cotton

DRAFTING STEPS

1 Trace the torso slopers onto a separate piece of paper. If you added a bust dart for your sloper, fold and tape down before tracing, since plenty of ease will be added. Make sure to leave enough room around the traced pieces to make modifications and add seam allowances.

2 Modify front sloper.

a. Extend shoulder by 4 inches, following the slope of the shoulder.

b. About 3 inches below the bottom of the armhole, draw a horizontal line approximately 1½ inches in length. Connect the endpoints of the extended shoulder and underarm horizontal line. Drape against your body to make sure your arm will fit.

c. Lengthen hem by about 3 inches.

d. Extend hem width to about the same as 2b. Draw a line upwards to connect to about the middle of the horizontal line (2b).

e. Curve underarm.

f. Square corners and curve hems (see page 72).

g. Curve the center front edge starting at the shoulder to about halfway down the center line. This will be the neck opening.

3 Modify back sloper.

a. If using Swedish tracing paper or another kind of sheer material, place traced back sloper on top of the modified front piece, aligning the shoulders. Trace the extended shoulder, side, and hem. Alternatively, repeat steps a–f from front sloper modifications.

STEPS 2 + 3

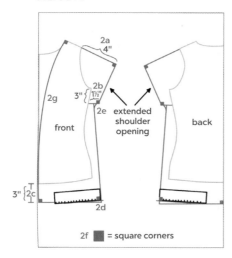

4 Draft sleeve.

a. Measure the extended shoulder opening of the front piece, which will be the new armhole. Draw a vertical line on the folded paper with that measurement.

b. Bend your arm slightly and measure the distance between your shoulder and your wrist bone with a measuring tape (I find it helpful to secure the end of the measuring tape with washi or clear tape to my wrist). Subtract the amount you added to the shoulder width in step 2a, which was 4 inches in my case. This will be your sleeve length. Mark this distance from 4a along the fold.

c. Measure your wrist circumference (if you don't already have this recorded), divide the number in half, and add about 2 inches for the sleeve hem. Draw a vertical line from the 4b marking with this measurement.

d. Connect the endpoints of the vertical lines.

e. Draw a line 1 inch up from the sleeve hem for the sleeve lining (the sleeve lining will be shorter). You'll be adding seam allowance to this, so don't cut the sleeve pattern out yet.

f. Square corners (see page 72).

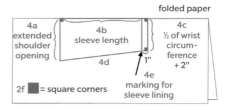

5 Draft pocket. Place a piece of tracing paper on top of the front piece, and trace the lower section. Draw a diagonal line for the pocket opening. Mine was 14 inches high at the center (measured from the bottom of the center edge along the front opening) and 5½ inches high at the side (measured from the bottom of the outer edge along the side).

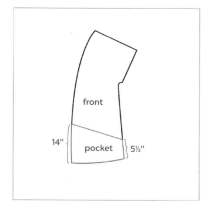

STEP 6

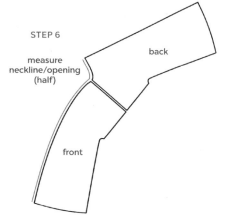

7 Draft collar. Draw a rectangle with a width of 4 inches and the length determined in step 6, your half neckline/opening measurement, plus ¾ inch. If you'd like, you could also draft the collar directly on the fabric.

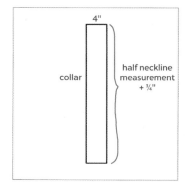

6 Place the pattern pieces with shoulders aligned and measure the neckline from back to front and continuing all the way down to the hem. Record this number (I like to write it on the front pattern piece). Keep in mind that this is half of the neckline measurement, which is what you will need for drafting the collar later, so you will not need to double it as you would with some of the other patterns.

8 Draft the back lining piece. Trace the entire center back line and the lower part of the back piece up to the underarm (the horizontal aqua line in the illustration). Then pivot the back piece counterclockwise ½ inch away from the center fold line. Trace the upper part of the back, connecting the underarm and extending the neckline to the center fold line. This extra amount will become a pleat.

trace up to this line on this side

back

pivot and trace upper portion

½"

center fold line

back

this part will become an inverted box pleat

back lining

9 Align the pattern pieces and make adjustments as needed (see page 67). Cut out pattern pieces, leaving plenty of room to add seam allowances.

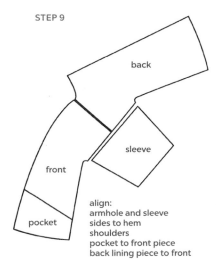

back

sleeve

front

pocket

align:
armhole and sleeve
sides to hem
shoulders
pocket to front piece
back lining piece to front

10 Add seam allowance as shown (see page 67). Cut pattern pieces at seam allowance, label and add grainline (see page 48) and markings. Make sure to mark the pocket positions on the front pieces. For the back lining, mark the pleat position. The sleeve lining will be 1 inch shorter than the sleeve.

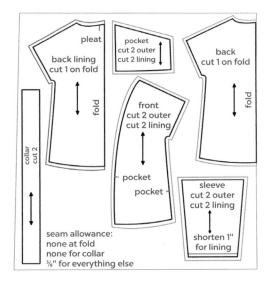

pleat

back lining
cut 1 on fold

pocket
cut 2 outer
cut 2 lining

back
cut 1 on fold

collar
cut 2

front
cut 2 outer
cut 2 lining

fold

fold

pocket

pocket

sleeve
cut 2 outer
cut 2 lining

shorten 1"
for lining

seam allowance:
none at fold
none for collar
⅜" for everything else

sewing love

CONSTRUCTION STEPS

1 Place pattern pieces on outer (shell) and lining fabrics, trace, and cut out. Remember that the sleeve lining is 1 inch shorter than the outer sleeve.

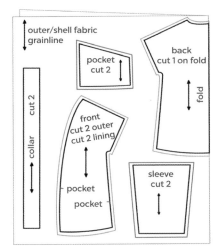

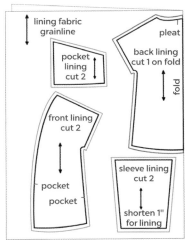

2 Optional: iron fusible interfacing to wrong side of outer pocket pieces at angled edges. Alternatively, staystitch (see page 51) both shell and lining pieces about ¼ inch from edge.

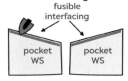

3 Attach pockets.

a. With right sides together, sew corresponding pocket and lining with a ⅜-inch seam allowance along top diagonal edge. Trim *lining* seam allowance only to about ¼ inch.

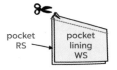

b. Flip lining over and press. Edgestitch ⅛ inch from folded edge along diagonal. Repeat with other pocket and lining. Press.

c. Baste pocket onto the corresponding front piece. Repeat for other pocket. Optional: to prevent pockets from gaping open, sew the pocket partially closed at the center front or from the side edge. Sew over existing edgestitching about 5 inches from center front or side.

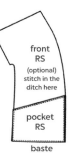

sewing love

4 Sew shoulders. With right sides together, align shoulders of shell front and back pieces and sew with a ⅜-inch seam allowance. Press seam allowances open.

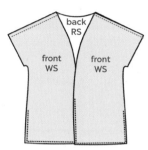

5 Attach sleeves. With right sides together, attach sleeves with a ⅜-inch seam allowance. Press seam allowances toward sleeve.

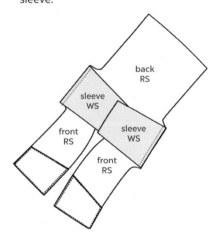

6 Sew sleeves and sides. With right sides together, pin, then sew the bottom of the sleeve, pivot at armpit, and continue to sew down the side with a ⅜-inch seam allowance. Repeat for other sleeve and side. If the fabric puckers at the armpit area, clip into the corner at the bottom of the armhole (be careful not to cut into the seam!). Press seam allowances open.

STEP 6

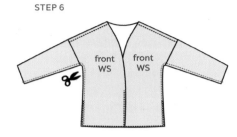

7 Attach collar.

a. Stitch the two collar pieces together along the short ends on one side with right sides facing and with a ⅜-inch seam allowance. Press seam allowance open. This seam will be at the back of the neckline.

b. Fold each end with right sides facing, and sew with a ⅜-inch seam allowance. Trim seam allowance to about ⅛ inch. Turn right side out and push the corners out.

c. Fold in half lengthwise with wrong sides together and press.

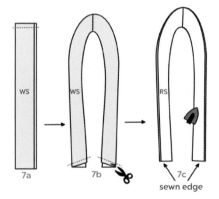

d. Attach collar. Align raw edges with the neckband on the right side of the jacket. Starting at the center back, pin collar all the way down each side of the center front. The coat shell should extend ⅜ inch below the collar at hem. Baste the collar to the coat with a ¼-inch seam allowance.

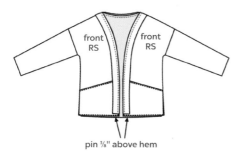

pin ⅜" above hem

8. Prepare back lining. With right sides together, sew 2–3 inches down from the pleat marking. Press the folded seam allowance open, flattening the fold behind the inverted pleat (see Skirt with Inverted Box Pleat, page 231). Baste the flattened fold about ¼ inch from the top edge.

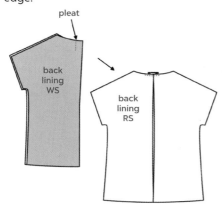

9. Sew lining. Repeat steps 4–6 for lining pieces, but leave an opening of about 5 inches in one of the side seams.

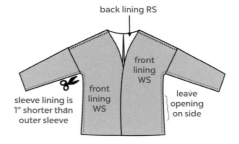

back lining RS

front lining WS

sleeve lining is 1" shorter than outer sleeve

front lining WS

leave opening on side

10. Bag the lining.

a. Pin lining to coat shell with right sides together. Starting at the bottom corner of the collar, sew with a ⅜-inch seam allowance all the way around the neckline and hem, making sure that the bottom edge of the collar doesn't get caught in the stitches. Clip corners and seam allowance curves along hem, neckline, and front opening.

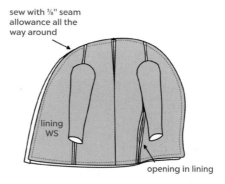

sew with ⅜" seam allowance all the way around

lining WS

opening in lining

b. Pull apart shell and lining as shown. Making sure that the sleeves aren't twisted, fold about 3 inches of the sleeve lining edge toward the wrong side and slip it into the corresponding shell sleeve (right sides facing).

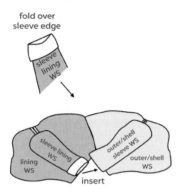

fold over
sleeve edge

sleeve lining WS

lining WS

sleeve lining WS

outer/shell sleeve WS

outer/shell WS

insert

c. Stitch the sleeve openings together with a ⅜-inch seam allowance, catching only 2 layers: one lining and one outer shell. This part can get confusing because you might try to sew all the layers together, but you are sewing just the sleeve edges.

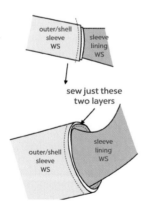

outer/shell sleeve WS

sleeve lining WS

sew just these two layers

outer/shell sleeve WS

sleeve lining WS

11 Turn coat right side out from lining opening. Keep pulling, pulling, pulling, gently pushing the sleeve lining into the sleeves (it's like magic!). Slip-stitch opening in lining closed. Topstitch along collar. Give it a good press and all done!

front RS

front RS

Variation: Flared Coat

FOR A SLEEKER TAKE ON this coat, switch to inseam pockets and omit the collar. Here the hem is widened a bit more, and I'm introducing a slash-and-spread technique to create a bell shape for the sleeve, which is a good one to have in your toolkit. You can apply this technique to skirt and pant hems, necklines, and so much more to add flare and flair! Optional: if you want a closure of some type, a ribbon or cord is a cinch to add.

MODIFICATIONS

- In drafting step 2d, extend the hem width to about 3 inches beyond the sloper hem and draw an angled line to connect to 2b.
- In drafting step 2g, add about 1 inch to the front curved edge and extend all the way down to the hem.

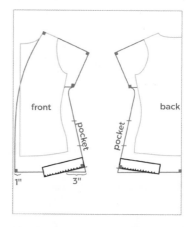

EXTRA SUPPLIES + MATERIALS

Optional: 2 pieces ribbon or cord, approx. 15 inches each

- Create a bell sleeve.
  a. After you've drafted the sleeve in draft-
     ing step 4, unfold the sleeve pattern
     and use the slash-and-spread method
     to flare it out. Divide the sleeve edge
     into four roughly equal segments and
     draw parallel lines upward, stopping ¼
     inch from the top of the sleeve. Place
     a piece of paper larger than the sleeve
     underneath, then spread the segments
     apart by ½ inch. Tape to secure.

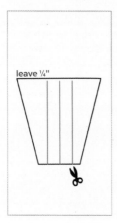

leave ¼"

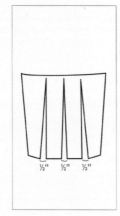

½"   ½"   ½"

- Measure an additional 1½ inches horizontally out from the bottom edge of each
  sleeve, then draw a line up to intersect
  about a third of the way up the sleeve.
  Smooth out angles into a curve and square corners.
- Add seam allowance as shown.

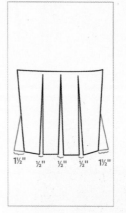

1½" ½" ½" ½" 1½"

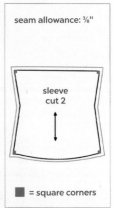

seam allowance: ⅜"

sleeve
cut 2

■ = square corners

- Skip drafting step 5 and trace pocket
  template from page 259 instead.
- Align pattern pieces per drafting step 6,
  but skip the collar measurement and all of
  drafting step 7 (collar).
- In construction step 3, instead of
  attaching the front pockets, follow
  inseam pocket instructions for the
  Sleeveless Dress with Pockets, page 157.
  Don't worry about finishing raw edges, as
  they will be encased in the coat lining.
- Skip construction step 6, but make sure
  to sew inseam pockets.
- Optional: in construction step 7, baste
  ribbon or cord pieces to the right side of
  the front piece where the curve begins.
- As a final step, topstitch along neckline
  and front opening, if desired.

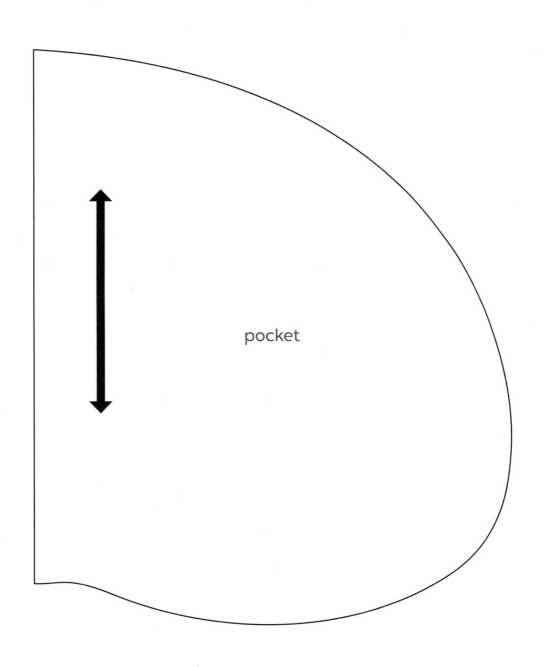

pocket

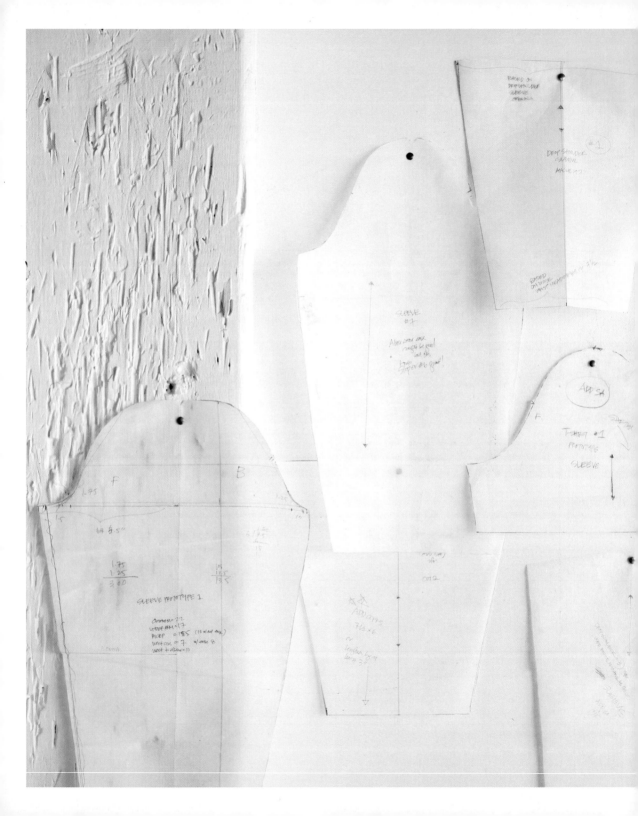

Acknowledgments

WHAT A TREMENDOUS ADVENTURE this book has been! I want to thank every single person involved, but I will have to limit my outpouring of gratitude to this page.

Thank you to . . .

First, Hannah Elnan, my amazing editor; Anna Goldstein, the equally amazing art director; and Bridget Sweet, the amazingly meticulous and lovely production editor. I am grateful for the entire staff at Sasquatch Books for making my dreams come true again and again.

Karen LePage, my sewing fairy godmother. Many thanks for hand-crafting the beautiful clothes for the beautiful models.

The best photo team ever: Manuela Insixiengmay, Rachel Grunig, Amy Johnson, and Kaija Towner, plus Lauren Segal who added her own magic.

The loveliest models: Wendee, Mimi, Melizza, Amy, Natasha, Rachel, M, and K. You made the clothes and book come alive!

The generous testers: over one hundred people tested the slopers and projects, and any errors still remaining are all my own. Your feedback was invaluable.

Natasha Alphonse, for the sublime ceramic pieces featured in the book.

Kiko Waters of The Cura Co., for the on-point styling help and accessories.

My Patreon members, who continued to encourage me forward. As always, I am sending you so much love.

My entire family: M and K and K, you are my loves.

Last but not least, Annelieke Schauer, to whom this book is dedicated. You are my creative kindred spirit. Yaaaaass, queen!

Thank you, thank you, thank you. How appropriate that this book is called *Sewing Love*, because it's been fueled from beginning to end by love.

Resources

I HAVE AN OUTRAGEOUS NUMBER of books on sewing and fitting and have listed quite a few of them (but not all!) below. Since they are reference books, I tend to forage through various books to look for ideas or solutions. They are listed alphabetically by title, and I have added an asterisk (*) next to my favorites. Although I've broken them down into different categories, there will be some overlap in terms of designing patterns and fitting in many of the books.

ABOUT FABRICS

All New Fabric Savvy by Sandra Betzina

Fabrics and Pattern Cutting by Winifred Aldrich

ABOUT FITTING

Create the Perfect Fit by Joi Mahon

Dressmaking for Real Women by Lorna Knight

Fantastic Fit for Everybody by Gale Grigg Hazen

* *Fast Fit* by Sandra Betzina

First Time Garment Fitting by Sarah Veblen

Fit for Real People by Pati Palmer and Marta Alto

Fitting and Pattern Alteration by Elizabeth Liechty, Judith Rasband, and
    Della Pottberg-Steineckert

Pattern Fitting with Confidence by Nancy Zieman

Perfectly Fitted by Lynne Garner

* *SEW . . . The Garment-Making Book of Knowledge* by Barbara Emodi

* *The Complete Photo Guide to Perfect Fitting* by Sarah Veblen
The Palmer/Pletsch Complete Guide to Fitting by Pati Palmer and
  Marta Alto
Vogue Sewing by Crystal McDonald

ABOUT PATTERN DRAFTING AND DESIGNING
* *Designing Clothes with the Flat Pattern Method* by Sarah Alm
* *How to Design Your Own Dress Patterns* by Adele P. Margolis
* *How to Make Sewing Patterns* by Don McCunn
How to Use, Adapt and Design Sewing Patterns by Lee Hollahan
Pattern Cutting Made Easy by Gillian Holman
Pattern Design Fundamentals by Jennifer Lynne Matthews-Fairbanks
*Patternmaking for Fashion Design by Helen Joseph Armstrong
The Pattern Making Primer by Jo Barnfield and Andrew Richards

ONLINE SEWING AND FITTING CLASSES AND RESOURCES
Craftsy: Craftsy.com
Creativebug: Creativebug.com
Ikat Bag Blog: IkatBag.com
In-House Patterns: InHousePatterns.com
Skillshare: Skillshare.com

Index

Conversions

SEAM ALLOWANCES

⅛ inch = 3 mm	⅝ inch = 1.6 cm
¼ inch = 6 mm	¾ inch = 2 cm
⅜ inch = 1 cm	⅞ inch = 2.3 cm
½ inch = 1.3 cm	1 inch = 2.5 cm

YARDAGE

¼ yard = 23 cm	1¼ yard = 1.2 m	2¼ yards = 2.1 m
½ yard = 45 cm	1½ yard = 1.4 m	2½ yards = 2.3 m
¾ yard = 70 cm	1¾ yards = 1.6 m	2¾ yards = 2.5 m
1 yard = 90 cm	2 yards = 1.8 m	3 yards = 2.7 m

Note: These conversions are rounded approximations. For more accurate conversions, use the Conversion Guide that follows.

CONVERSION GUIDE

FROM	TO	MULTIPLY BY
Inches	Centimeters	2.54
Feet	Meters	0.305
Yards	Meters	0.915